SpringerBriefs on Pioneers in Science and Practice

Volume 37

Series editor

Hans Günter Brauch, Mosbach, Germany

More information about this series at http://www.springer.com/series/10970
http://www.afes-press-books.de/html/SpringerBriefs_PSP.htm
http://afes-press-books.de/html/SpringerBriefs_PSP_Rummel.htm

Nils Petter Gleditsch

Editor

R.J. Rummel: An Assessment of His Many Contributions

Editor
Nils Petter Gleditsch
Peace Research Institute Oslo (PRIO)
Oslo
Norway

Acknowledgement: The cover photograph and other photos in this book are family pictures provided by Rummel's daughter Dawn Akemi.
The editor acknowledges technical assistance from Marie Iselin Bjerkelund.
A book website with additional information on Rummel is found at: http://afes-press-books. de/html/SpringerBriefs_PSP_Rummel.htm. A website with additional information on the editor, Prof. Nils Petter Gleditsch, and his two affiliations at PRIO in Oslo and at NTNU in Trondheim, Norway is at: http://afes-press-books.de/html/SpringerBriefs_PSP_Gleditsch.htm. A webpage with a backup of Rummel's homepage at the University of Hawaii and an errata sheet for this volume can be found at www.prio.org/RummelAssessment.
In order to access pages on Rummel's website, it is essential to use CAPITAL LETTERS where specified in the web address.

ISSN 2194-3125   ISSN 2194-3133   (electronic)
SpringerBriefs on Pioneers in Science and Practice
ISBN 978-3-319-54462-5   ISBN 978-3-319-54463-2   (eBook)
DOI 10.1007/978-3-319-54463-2

Library of Congress Control Number: 2017934628

Copyediting: PD Dr. Hans Günter Brauch, AFES-PRESS e.V., Mosbach, Germany

Printed on acid-free paper

This Springer imprint is published by Springer Nature
The registered company is Springer International Publishing AG
The registered company address is: Gewerbestrasse 11, 6330 Cham, Switzerland

Foreword

I will not attempt here a review of Rudy's full career and corpus. The chapters to follow accomplish that goal well. Rather, I offer a preface to his career, from my experience as his assistant professor colleague at Yale during the 2 years from 1964 to 1966, in the hope that experience may shed light on his later development. We were then beneficiaries of Karl Deutsch's pioneering NSF grant to produce and analyze cross-national political and social data. Dick Merritt and Hayward Alker were also involved. But by 1964 I had my own NSF grant, and Rudy brought his own NSF grant to Yale to establish his Dimensionality of Nations project. With Karl, Dick, Hayward, and Rudy no longer on this earth, I feel a bit like Ishmael citing Job 1:13 to begin his Epilogue to *Moby Dick:* 'I only am escaped alone to tell thee.'

All of us were number crunchers to one degree or another, and Yale was an Ivy League university with no assured tenure track. So it was clear that the Political Science Department would be unable, or unwilling, to tenure more than one or two of us. The situation was objectively very competitive, yet we all maintained good relations with one another. Rudy was particularly co-operative, and was eager to share his knowledge of factor analysis—a fine colleague. Yet he was, as he admits in his biography, something of a loner, and all the other three were Yale PhDs of approximately the same vintage. We were also well known to most members of the Department, which was mostly advantageous. I was probably his best friend in the Department, and I have good memories of the times Cynthia and I had dinner with Rudy and his wife Grace. One time, shortly after we had moved into our new house, they brought a potted holly tree, and we planted it next to the house. It is now a tree reaching above the roofline, and I often think of them when I care for it.

If Rudy had any hope of staying at Yale, he was not very strategic about it. The Department sponsored lunches for all faculty at Mory's—a quintessential old boy hangout. The rest of us often attended, but Rudy quickly determined that the conversation was not worth his time, and quit going. Rudy was there long enough to get into a conversation with a new senior comparativist who immediately established himself as a mover and shaker. He had an up-from-the-streets background, and ethnically was part of an honor culture. He inquired about Rudy's work with increasing skepticism, especially about fancy statistical analysis. Rudy tried his best, but with little success. Finally he said, within hearing distance of others, 'You just don't understand factor analysis.' I watched the senior member's face, and knew that his honor had been challenged. Rudy had moved him from a position of relative neutrality to determined opposition. Rudy had weak social skills, and was quite open about it. In 1966 the Department tried to promote Hayward but he was a free spirit and went to MIT instead, and Dick went to the University of Illinois. Yale promoted me to associate professor. This settled most of the competition questions, but it did not mean Rudy could expect our Department to promote him. About the same time he was offered a professorship at the University of Hawaii, where he had done his BA. He loved Hawaii, and was very pleased to go back. And he never left. So I think that pull was greater than Yale's likely push.

I read, and still read, some science fiction, but Rudy was an avid fan. He quickly told me about his favorite, Isaac Asimov's *Foundation Trilogy* published in 1951, 1952, and 1953. Hari Seldon, the protagonist, chiefly of the first volume, is a mathematician and creator of the science of psychohistory. Seldon gathered the best minds to predict future macrohistory—the big patterns, not the details of time and space for particular events and personalities. It was nonetheless a practical science devoted to saving the universe from chaos and war. Seldon was a model scientist, a genius, and Rudy's fictional hero. A reader of Rudy's work can readily see the similarities. Don't, however, picture Rudy as arrogant or too egotistic. He had great integrity, ceasing teaching because he couldn't hear his students well enough. But he was a highly intelligent man with great imagination and breadth of academic and artistic talents. And he knew that. He also had great drive, evident in the enormous volume of published work requiring extensive research, analysis, and entrepreneurship. He was doing his part to save the world from war and chaos.

His work largely wears well. *Death by Government* detailed the human horrors of absolute states. He deserves credit for finding elements of what became known as the Democratic Peace, and bits of the Kantian Peace (his libertarian belief in free domestic and international markets). But I don't think he fully comprehended what he had found, as his political ideal was not simply democracy as later characterized by institutions on a Polity scale. He used the adjective libertarian to indicate a small and tightly restrained government, favoring individual liberty and free enterprise.[1] I think that led to his depiction of the Soviet Union as an implacable enemy to be restrained only by the threat and use of military force. The irony is that he didn't understand the policy implications of his extremely hawkish views. He did not consider all the real policy implications of following his controversial policy, notably the effect of sustained confrontation in producing what Harold Lasswell back in 1941 called 'The Garrison State'. A garrison state means a militarized state

---

[1]A libertarian friend, whom I considered an ally in opposing the Vietnam War and other foreign entanglements, characterized his own position simply as 'Get the government off my back, and out of my crotch'.

and society—not a libertarian country. We see elements of a garrison state now in a militarized culture, a military-industrial complex, and great governmental power to intensely monitor individuals' activity. Rudy missed this one …

Bruce Russett
Yale University, New Haven, CT, USA

Bruce Russett b. 1935, Ph.D. in political science (Yale, 1961) is Dean Acheson research professor of political science at Yale University and former chair of the Department of Political Science. He served as President of the Peace Science Society (International) in 1977–79 and the International Studies Association in 1983–84. His most recent book is *Hegemony and Democracy* (Norton, 2011). Harvey Starr has edited a biography, *Bruce M Russett: Pioneer in the Scientific and Normative Study of War, Peace, and Policy* (Springer, 2015).

Contents

Self portrait of R.J. Rummel downloaded from his website at: http://www.hawaii.edu/powerkills/
PERSONAL.HTM and http://www.hawaii.edu/powerkills/GALLERY3.HTM

General Young-ok Park, Grace Rummel, Rudy Rummel, and Sang-Woo Rhee—in Waikiki, Oahu,
Hawaii in 2003. From Rhee's private photo collection

Chapter 1
R.J. Rummel—A Multi-faceted Scholar

Nils Petter Gleditsch

Rudolph J. Rummel always published just as R.J. Rummel but was well known in the profession as Rudy.[1] He was a man of many talents, and to some of his readers he may also have seemed to present many different faces. He came from a broken home, yet became a devoted husband and father. He had an extensive academic publication record, but he also wrote six novels. He was an academic loner, but acquired a wide following, which has continued to expand after he withdrew from the academic scene and promises to continue to grow even after his death. He interacted with many leading scholars in international relations, but developed troubled relations with several. He started out as a socialist but became a libertarian or, as he himself eventually phrased it, a freedomist. He became a pioneer among liberal international relations scholars in his pursuit of the democratic peace, but he joined the neoconservative wing of the realists in his work on the nuclear arms race in the mid-1970s and in his support for the Iraq War in 2003. His work on democide was embraced by liberals and realists alike, but also harshly criticized by writers of varying backgrounds.

Nils Petter Gleditsch, b. 1942, Research professor at the Peace Research Institute Oslo (PRIO), and Professor emeritus of political science at the Norwegian University of Science and Technology (NTNU), former editor (1983–2010) of *Journal of Peace Research*. Former President of the International Studies Association (2008–09); Email: nilspg@prio.org.

[1]Most of the chapters in this book originated in a roundtable at the 56th Convention of the *International Studies Association* (ISA), New Orleans, LA, 18–21 February 2015. I am particularly grateful to Doug Bond for his assistance in setting up the roundtable and his encouragement and help throughout the book project. Valuable comments were received from the authors of the following chapters as well as from Scott Gates, Kristian Skrede Gleditsch, Warren R. Phillips, Bruce Russett, Jonathan Wilkenfeld, and Dina Zinnes. Finally, I acknowledge the financial support of the Research Council of Norway and the Gløbius Fund for supporting my work on the introduction and the editing and open-access publication of the volume.

© The Author(s) 2017
N.P. Gleditsch (ed.), *R.J. Rummel: An Assessment of His Many Contributions*,
SpringerBriefs on Pioneers in Science and Practice 37,
DOI 10.1007/978-3-319-54463-2_1

The main aim of this book is to review his work and to assess the development of his views over the span of his career. At the same time, several contributors relate his academic and political views to his personal life story. The authors of this volume share the view that despite what quibbles or even quarrels they might have with some of his writings, Rummel stands as a very significant contributor to the empirical and theoretical study of human conflict. At the same time, he was an intensely political person who has influenced the moral compass of many scholars in the profession.

1.1   A Rummel Timeline

On two occasions, Rummel (1976b, 1989) has provided autobiographical accounts. The story of his checkered childhood and youth emerges here, as well as in his daughter's recollections (Chap. 2) and Doug Bond's interview with him (Chap. 3). Here, he also talks at length about his shifting research interests and his increasing unease with socialist ideology. I will attempt a very broad periodization of Rummel's professional work.

From the start of his education, Rummel embraced mathematics—apparently, a youthful interest in science fiction influenced this choice. Indeed, his first academic work was heavily mathematical, with empirical studies of conflict and a major textbook on factor analysis (Rummel, 1970). But, as Richard Chadwick explains (Chap. 5), for Rummel factor analysis was not just a methodological tool but also a key part of a theoretical framework that came to be known as social field theory. While many other scholars adopted and elaborated empirical findings that emerged from these projects, in particular those relating to the relationship between internal and external conflict, few others attributed the same theoretical importance to factor analysis. Nevertheless, Rummel's reputation as a quantitative scholar of note grew rapidly in the scholarly community and in policy circles. He received extensive funding from the US Department of Defense, through the Advanced Research Projects Agency (ARPA),[2] which funded a number of conflict research projects in the 1960s and 1970s. Rummel's projects, in particular the large Dimensionality of Nations (DON) Project, also involved substantial data collection, and the data were used by a wide range of scholars.

A second phase of Rummel's work started when, according to his own recollections (Rummel, 1989: 314) he took a step back from data collection and hypothesis-testing to look at the broader theoretical preconditions and implications of his work. He started what he has called an 'intensive and extensive liberal self-education' in philosophy, history, and the social sciences. This eventually led to the massive oeuvre collectively titled *Understanding Conflict and War*, published in

---

[2]From 1972 (and again in 1996) renamed the Defense Advanced Research Projects Agency (DARPA), cf. http://www.darpa.mil. The vast majority of ARPA-supported projects were technical and weapons-oriented. ARPA is probably best known for its development of the ARPANET, which eventually became the Internet.

Kaneohe, Oahu, Hawaii, where Rummel lived most of the time in Hawaii and Kaneohe Bay where he now rests. Photo from personal photo collection of his family

five volumes between 1975 and 1981. The series title was apparently proposed by Sage, but in retrospect Rummel regretted agreeing to this series title, since it only really fit vol. 4 (*War, Power, Peace,* 1979). As James Lee Ray argues (Chap. 8), it is in many ways an overlooked classic. Rummel himself, while not expecting it to be a hit, was unprepared for its being so widely ignored. The sales were poor. Only a few years later, an article in *Journal of Conflict Resolution* (Rummel, 1983a) was to change the landscape dramatically. This article, along with a two-part article by Doyle (1983), launched the democratic peace on the mainstream agendas of peace research and international relations. A number of other scholars joined in, notably Bruce Russett and Zeev Maoz.[3] Rummel once again became a household name.

A few years later, the debate was extended to a broader liberal peace, involving the Kantian triangle of democracy, economic interdependence, and international orga-nization. This line of investigation was initiated by Oneal, Oneal, Maoz & Russett (1996) and is primarily associated with Bruce Russett and John Oneal, in a series of frequently-cited articles and a book (Russett & Oneal, 2001). Rummel (1976a) had expressed skepticism about the peacebuilding effects of trade and international organizations (cf. Chap. 6). He did not enter the new debate about the liberal peace, which started after he had retired from the university and stopped publishing articles in academic journals. His 1983 article on the democratic peace—and indeed, in his four subsequent articles indexed by Web of Science between 1984 and 1986—referred to libertarianism rather than democracy. The same is true of *Understanding Conflict and War.* Libertarian was defined along two dimensions, political (where, of course, democracy featured prominently) and economic. In his articles on libertari-anism and international violence, the term democratic peace does not occur at all.

---

[3]See, in particular, Maoz & Russett (1993) and Russett (1993).

Rummel playing tennis. Photo from personal photo collection of his family

In his later work, however, even as the attention of the field moved to broader aspects of the liberal peace, Rummel focused on democracy. On his website,[4] democratic peace is one of the main headlines. In some ways, his work can be seen as a precursor of the more recent discussion of the capitalist peace (cf. Weede in Chap. 7, Gartzke, 2007). But as far as I have been able to ascertain, Rummel himself never used the term capitalist peace, and his work was sometimes critical of unbridled capitalism or liberalism.[5] From 2009, his blog was labelled freedomist rather than libertarian. And his two final books were called *The Blue Book of Freedom* (2007) and *Freedom's Principles* (2008).

Although Rummel's work on the democratic peace focused mainly on the interstate democratic peace, he also eventually concluded that 'democracies are most internally peaceful', that 'democracies don't murder their citizens',[6] and that democratic freedom promotes wealth and prosperity and prevents famines.[7] It was the latter point that was going to lead Rummel into a new phase of his work and another major series of books on what he came to call democide, a concept that was deliberately chosen to be wider than genocide and politicide. Separate volumes examined the Soviet Union (1990), China (1991), and Nazi Germany (1992), before he summed it all up in *Death by Government* (1994) and *Statistics of Democide* (1997). In *Power Kills* (1997), he tied together his work on democracy and the various kinds of human conflict. The subtitle of this book was Democracy as a Method of Nonviolence. It underscored Rummel's long-standing commitment to a less violent world, even though as Erica Chenoweth points out (Chap. 11) he never commented directly on non-violent action as a substitute for insurgency and war.

---

[4]See at. https://www.hawaii.edu.powerkills.MIRACLE.HTM.

[5]Cf. Rummel (1976d: Chap. 22, 1981: Chap. 2).

[6]Chapter headings in Rummel (1997).

[7]Rummel (2007: Chap. 6).

One of his Ph.D. students nonetheless studied this topic in his dissertation, with the use of factor analysis! (Bond, 1988).

The work on democide is probably the aspect of Rummel's work that captures most attention now. It was also to be his last major research effort even though he continued to publish shorter articles, blog posts—and six novels, to which I return briefly later.

In this brief attempt at a periodization of Rummel's work, I have omitted a book that does not fall clearly into any of the major periods. This is his book on the nuclear arms race, discussed in this volume by Matthew Kroenig & Bardia Rahmani (Chap. 6). In *Peace Endangered: Reality of Détente* (1976a), Rummel critiqued détente, expressed skepticism about arms control, and called for a policy that would give the West a clear nuclear superiority over the Soviet Union. Published at a time when liberals were hopeful about détente and arms control, it created a significant distance between himself and scholars who might have been receptive to his message about freedom and peace. Instead, it probably reinforced the prejudice, still common in peace research, that talking about a democratic peace just meant rehashing old enemy images of 'us' and 'them' and familiar propaganda for 'the free world'. Richard Chadwick notes in an aside (Chap. 5, note 2) an estrangement between Rummel and himself. It dates to this period, though not exclusively to this issue. Intriguingly, Rummel relates (1989: 317f) that his hawkish message was not well received in the national security establishment either, which led to a cut-off of his long-term funding from DARPA.

1.2   The Lone Ranger

Rummel's extensive writings are listed in Chap. 13 of this book. His work is frequently cited, and remains influential nearly two decades after he withdrew from academic publishing. Figure 1.1 shows the number of citations to his articles indexed in Web of Science for the past fifty years. Using the Author file, the total number of citations to his articles as of mid-August 2016, was 797. The overall regression line is obviously positive. But we can spot three humps in the annual citation rate. The first (which peaks in 1972) relates to his early work on methods and on the relationship between internal and external conflict. The next hump peaks in 1997 and is probably linked to the democratic peace, although a more detailed analysis would be necessary to establish this conclusively. The final peak, which is also the peak for the whole time series, occurs in 2007, and includes citations to his work on democide. However, it is not the case that his earlier work remains uncited in later periods. In fact, his 1967 factor analysis article has been cited more than 20 times since 2010.

Table 1.1 shows his most-cited articles. This table was compiled from the Cited authors file of Web of Science rather than from the Author file. A Basic search on Author yields lower numbers because it does not include periodicals not indexed by WoS in that year (such as the *European Journal of International Relations* before 1997) and because a number of citations are not correctly linked to the relevant article. The discrepancies between the numbers derived from the Author and Cited

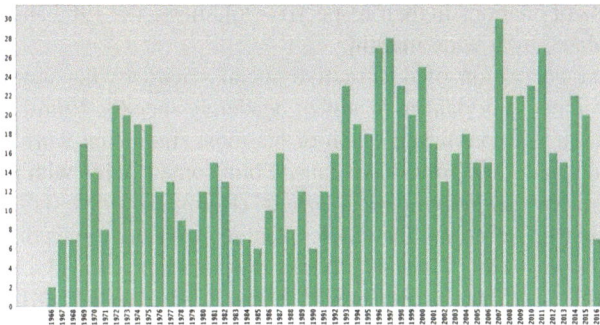

Fig. 1.1 Citations to Rummel's articles, 1966–2016 *Source* Downloaded with permission from the author file at *Web of Science*, 18 August 2016. © Copyright Thomson Reuters (2016). All rights reserved. For a description of the limitations of this file to assess the total citations of an author, see below in the main text. Apart from a brief comment (Rummel, 2004a, b) the last WoS-indexed article by Rummel appeared in print in 1997

Table 1.1 Citations to Rummel's ten most-cited journal articles, 1966–2015

1	Understanding factor analysis, JCR (1967)	228
2	Dimensions of conflict behavior within and between nations, GSY (1963)	205
3	Libertarianism and international violence, JCR (1983)	202
4	Democracy, power, genocide, and mass murder, JCR (1995)	87
5	Democracies ARE less warlike than other regimes, EJIR (1995	75
6	Dimensions of conflict behavior within nations, 1946–59, JCR (1966)	72
7	Libertarian propositions on violence within and between nations ..., JCR (1985)	69
8	A field theory of social action with application to conflict ..., GSY (1965)	61
9	How multinationals analyze political risk (with DA Heenan), HBR (1978)	40
10	Is collective violence correlated with social pluralism? JPR (1997)	38

Source Statistics from Web of Science, downloaded 26 August 2015. GSY = *General Systems: Yearbook of the Society for General Systems*, HBR = *Harvard Business Review*, JCR = *Journal of Conflict Resolution*, JPR = *Journal of Peace Research*. Articles in *American Political Science Review* (1969) and *World Politics* (1969), as well as several other articles in *Journal of Peace Research* (1966, 1967, 1994) were among those that fell just short of the top-ten list. Another article close to the top ten was on the DON project in *Comparing Nations* (1969), a volume edited by Richard Merritt & Stein Rokkan (Rummel, 1966)

author files are larger for the earlier years, when citation data were hand-coded from the print journals, apparently with little if any proofreading.

Table 1.1 underlines the wide impact of Rummel's work on factor analysis as well as the importance of *Journal of Conflict Resolution* throughout his career. Half the top-cited articles appeared in that journal. The close personal relationship between Rummel and Bruce Russett is only partly relevant here, since two of the top articles were published before Russett took over as editor of *JCR* in 1972. In turn, Rummel's authorship was probably important to the reputation of the journal, too. All the five Rummel articles listed here were among the top five articles in terms of citations in their respective volumes—the 1967 and 1983 articles were in first place, by a wide margin.

For the next generation of quantitative social scientists, the number of article citations is the most important indicator of academic success. Rummel was a more traditional scholar who published much of his most significant work in books. His somewhat contrarian stance may have caused him some trouble with journal editors and referees. In his autobiographical article (Rummel, 1989: 317), he hints at getting a number of rejections for articles dealing with the topics discussed in his book *Peace Endangered* (1976a). His books did not always travel a simple road to publication either, but nine books found a home at Sage (until 1981) and six with Transaction (from 1990). Table 1.2 lists citations to his most-frequently cited books, once again compiled from the Cited author file of Web of Science.

This list also underlines the wide impact of his work on factor analysis (as Ray suggests in Chap. 8). His factor analysis book was featured as a 'citation classic' in *Current Contents* (Rummel, 1987b). His more recent work on democide is also widely cited and has maintained high visibility in the current debate about the waning of war and violence. For instance, in his widely-cited book on the decline of violence, Pinker (2011) makes extensive use of Rummel's work on democide. Rummel's magnum opus *Understanding Conflict and War* is not as widely cited as one might expect. Because the books tend to be cited by the series title rather than by the volume title, I have not attempted to provide individual citation data for the five volumes. The importance of Rummel's books is also made clear by the fact that he has five times as many citations as Cited author than as Author, whereas comparable scholars like Johan Galtung and Bruce Russett have more citations as Author, because their articles are so widely cited.[8]

Another striking thing about Tables 1.1 and 1.2 is that Rummel has extremely limited co-authorship. Only one co-authored article just barely makes into the top-ten article list, and he has no co-authored books. By contrast, leading scholars of the same generation such as Johan Galtung, J. David Singer, and Bruce Russett have numerous co-authored articles and books. Co-authorship, although much less frequent than in the natural sciences where articles can have several hundred co-authors, is becoming increasingly common in the social sciences. In the earlier volumes of *Journal of Peace Research,* for instance, the average number of authors per article is generally between 1.1 and 1.3 (indicating that on average every third to every tenth article has a co-author, since few articles have more than two authors), rising to an average of nearly 2 for the most recent volumes.[9]

One plausible reason why Rummel has few co-authors is that as his daughter reminds us in Chap. 2, he was a rather private person and perhaps not temperamentally

---

[8]The reader may wonder how it is possible to have more citation to Author than to Cited author, when the latter includes all works, including books, whereas the first includes only WoS-indexed articles. The reason is that the Author file counts all article citations individually, whereas in the Cited author file the scholar only gets a single citation from an article that cites several of his/her works.

[9]I am grateful to my colleague Jonas Nordkvelle for compiling these statistics.

Table 1.2 Citations to Rummel's ten most-cited books, 1966–2015

1	Applied Factor Analysis (1970)	1,561
2	Death by Government (1994)	262
3	Understanding Conflict and War (1975–81)	149
4	Dimensions of Nations (1976c)	116
5	Power Kills (1997)	82
6	Lethal Politics: Soviet Genocides … (1990)	35
7	China's Bloody Century: Genocide … (1991)	30
8	Statistics of Democide (1997)	24
9	Democide: Nazi Genocide and Mass Murder (1992)	21
10	Field Theory Evolving (1977)	20

Source as in Table 1.1. The search was made on the Cited author file. The first book not to make it on to the list was *Peace Endangered* (1976a). Total number of citations on the Cited author file: 2,863

well suited to share the process of writing, although he maintained an active network of academic collaborators and contacts and frequently discussed his work with his students. He had a relatively low number of Ph.D. students. He was a very influential force in their professional lives, as Sang-Woo Rhee explains in Chap. 4, and Doug Bond describes him as the most supportive teacher he ever had.[10] Whether or not he encouraged or discouraged his students to publish while working on their dissertations is not entirely clear, but he certainly shared the prevailing notion that the dissertation had to come first. So did J. David Singer, but unlike Rummel he co-authored extensively, including with former students. And so did Russett and Galtung.

1.3   The Critics

Rummel's work has been subjected to extensive examination by other scholars, leading to praise as well as harsh criticism. The DON Project (along with three other major quantitative empirical projects in international relations) was subjected to close scrutiny in Hoole & Zinnes (1976), with separate chapters on the philosophy of science and research design of the project (Hilton, 1976), its methodology and statistical practices (Hazlewood, 1976), and the substantive findings (Van Atta & Robertson, 1976), in addition to a presentation and a bibliography by Rummel (1976d, f) and a brief response to the reviews (Rummel, 1976e). Hilton's chapter built on a detailed review of DON he had done earlier at Rummel's invitation (Hilton, 1973). It is impossible here to summarize all the specific points raised in these reviews. Some of them may have been bypassed by the rapid theoretical and empirical progress in social science since that time. Others, such as the role of theory in international relations research, how to deal with missing data, and the relative role of national attributes and relational characteristics in accounting for international interaction, remain.

---

[10]Personal communication, 9 October 2015.

Ray (1982, 1998, and Chap. 8) was always a constructive critic, who carefully read all five volumes of *Understanding Conflict and War*, which he characterized as one of the most energetic and comprehensive contributions to the scientific study of international relations. Despite criticism of many of Rummel's answers, he credited him with asking the right questions.

Another friendly critic was Warren R. Phillips, who had himself obtained his Ph.D. under Rummel and had served (1968–71) as assistant director of the DON Project. He was generally quite critical of the lack of theory in the international relations discipline but found Rummel's field theory to be a promising island of theory (Phillips, 1974). Several years later, he was more critical in reviewing *Peace Endangered*. While Rummel had done valuable work in mapping objective aspects of power (capabilities) his attempt to deal with the subjective aspects (interests and capability) were judged to be inadequate (Ensign & Phillips, 1980).

An equally well-read but more critical commentator was Wiberg (1982). While acknowledging the extraordinarily prolific nature of Rummel's scholarship, he criticized Rummel for the tautological nature of his comprehensive field theory, for biased summaries of some major schools in social science (such as frustration-aggression theory and Marxism), and particularly for questionable judgments in his wide-ranging literature review as to whether or not the empirical results from published articles support his theoretical framework, Rummel responded briefly (Rummel, 1983b) and later in a new article summarizing how published articles supported his libertarian propositions on violence (Rummel, 1985: 435, note 6).

Another strong critic was Vincent (1987a, b) who argued that Rummel's interdemocratic peace could not be sustained with an alternative set of conflict data. Rummel responded to this in the same journal issue. But Vincent used conflict data for only a few years in the 1970s, as did Rummel (1983a, b), which Vincent had critiqued. In view of the many analyses of the democratic peace using much longer time series for different well-established datasets, this debate is less relevant today. Rummel's long-time colleague at the University of Hawaii, Michael Haas, had found in an early article 'a slight but consistent tendency for democratic countries to have less foreign conflict' (Haas, 1965: 313), but later became a vocal critic of the democratic peace program (Haas, 2014).

Of great continuing interest is the debate about Rummel's democide estimates. Rummel created these on a country-by-country basis using published studies, concluding with three figures, a high estimate, a low estimate, and a most probable estimate. These could vary significantly. For the Soviet Union, for instance, Rummel (1990: 3) estimated a most probable democide of 62 million people, but with a range from 28 million to 127 million. In most of his work on democide, he focused on the most probable estimates, leaving himself somewhat vulnerable to criticism for excessive precision in these numbers. However, he also noted that he would be amazed if future research did not come up with figures that deviated significantly from his own. His figures should be viewed as rough approximations (Rummel, 1994: vii–xx).

His volume on the statistics of democide, however, as well as the books on the four 'deka-megamurderers' (the Soviet Union, China under Kuomintang, China under Mao, and Nazi Germany), contain all the sources and all the numbers and extensive comments on how he selected his own numbers. Some critics, including Harff (1996: 118) have argued that 'Rummel chooses numbers of deaths that almost always are skewed in the direction of the highest guesses'. In this volume, Barbara Harff (Chap. 12) cites but does not reiterate this criticism. Rather, in discussing Rummel's numbers for Cambodia, she finds that given his wide definition of democide, his estimates are consistent with established estimates in the literature and she also acknowledges his 'monumental job in collecting data and information'. A reviewer of Rummel's volume on democide in the Soviet Union chides him for not using Russian-language sources and for assuming citing a range of secondary sources 'as if they were all of equal worth'. He also faults Rummel for assuming 'that the entire labour camp population was innocent' although some of those who died in the camps 'were common criminals or actual Nazi collaborators' (Swain, 1991).

A critic of Rummel's democide estimates for Yugoslavia (Dulić, 2004a) argued, on the basis of considerable documentation, that Rummel's estimates for democide in Yugoslavia during World War II and in the immediate aftermath of the war were much too high. He also questioned whether similar data problems might occur in other democide estimates. Rummel (2004a, b) thanked him for his contribution to research on democide, but dismissed the overall claims of the critique, since Dulić had only commented on a portion of the time period covered by Rummel. Dulić (2004b) was not convinced.

As Rummel pointed out in his reply to Dulić, it is not enough to criticize the numbers he published. The issues are too important for criticism alone. Those who disagree with his numbers should feel a responsibility to come up with alternative and more reliable figures. Rummel's work on democide was not only a gigantic data collection effort, but also admirable in its transparency—long before the replication requirement became a standard feature of empirical work in international relations.

1.4   The Novelist and the Artist

Rummel's novels were written after he finished writing for academic journals and book publishers, but they are in direct continuity of the main themes from his research and were published under the general heading of the Never Again Series. I have only read the first (Rummel, 2004b), but that puts me ahead of most of the other contributors to this volume. The book is packed with love, sex, and action, and written in a rather macho style, quite common in its genre. The basic plot is that the hero, Rudolph Rummel himself in only a slight disguise, enters the past through a time-machine with a female partner, to create an alternative world where major wars and democides have been avoided. Through a mixture of bribery and assassinations, they derail the Mexican revolution, dispose of Hitler, Lenin, and Stalin long before

Rummel's caption: Dinner? Paintage. Well, it would be dinner if not for mother hen. The background was painted; and the chicks, hen, and two cats are each from separate photos I took around the outside of our house. Soon after this picture was made, all but two of these chicks disappeared—perhaps eaten by the cats. They are all wild animals that have taken to us, maybe because we feed them. *Source* https://www.hawaii.edu/powerkills/GAL2.CATS.CHICKS.HTM

they are anywhere near political power, and prevent the two World Wars as well as the Sino-Japanese War and the democide in China. One might wonder what is left to save the world from in the following volumes, but it appears that the time travelers ran into some unexpected future problems. Rummel's novels were probably too closely tied to his academic and political pursuits to stand much of a chance in the mass market of paperback fiction. The books are still available in electronic form from Llumina Press and from Rummel's website, and hard copies can be obtained from amazon.com. Llumina is a self-publishing press, and the publisher notes that sales of such books depend on the author's ability to promote and market them. In Rummel's cases, the sales were very limited.[11] Apart from their merits as fiction, the six novels reinforce the picture of an exceptionally diligent writer. Each book is 200–300 pages, and all six were published in a two-year period, along with a nonfiction supplement (Rummel, 2005).

Rummel was also an artist and in his later years spent a large part of his time painting. I am even less qualified to comment on his art than on his novels and happily defer to his daughter's comments in Chap. 2. An example of his art is found

---

[11]E-mail from Deborah Greenspan, Llumina Press, 17 November 2015.

on the previous page of this book and many others can be found at https://www.hawaii.edu/powerkills/GALLERY.HTM. But as someone who did know Rummel personally, I can testify that the self-portrait reproduced in front of this introduction is a good likeness. That brings me to a few final personal recollections.

1.5 Personal Recollections

I worked as research fellow for the Dimensionality of Nations Project in the spring of 1969. My visit had been arranged by correspondence between Johan Galtung and Rudy. At the time their relations were pleasant. Rummel was interested in Galtung's work relating status inconsistency to conflict (Galtung, 1964). Indeed, he actively tried to incorporate what he called status theory into his field theory (Rummel, 1971). But as H.-C. Peterson relates (Chap. 10), the cordiality got lost along the way. For many years they were colleagues in the Department of Political Science at the University of Hawaii. By this time, Galtung held the view that 'international relations US style' was bankrupt and when cut to pieces, it could be deconstructed as self-serving US ideology (Galtung, 1989: 166). Rummel, on the other hand, came to see Galtung's concept of structural violence as a socialist theory of peace within a neomarxist theory of exploitation (Rummel, 1981: 50, 83). The two colleagues hardly interacted. Rummel's relationship to Singer was much less acrimonious, although the two had a life-long disagreement on the prospects of explaining international relations, at least in part, on the basis of national indicators (cf. Wayman in Chap. 9). Rummel's particular mix of realism and liberalism, noted by Erich Weede in Chap. 7, may have made it difficult for him to form lasting alliances with other scholars.

Johan Galtung was my highly valued mentor, but over the years I came to rely more on Rummel's wisdom. As editor of *Journal of Peace Research*, I published the harsh critique of *Understanding Conflict and War* by Wiberg (1982), but my friendship with Rummel survived. I can recall two 'friendly quarrels' with Rummel. One was over his Nobel Peace Prize nomination. For years, Rummel had on his homepage that he had been shortlisted for the Nobel Peace Prize. Although the list of nominations is not made public by the Norwegian Nobel Committee, many nominators publicize their nominations and it was on record that Rummel had been nominated several times by former Swedish deputy prime minister Per Ahlmark. I tried to convince Rummel that the nomination itself was not necessarily such an unambiguous honor; indeed Adolf Hitler and Fidel Castro had also been nominated. Furthermore, there was absolutely no reliable evidence regarding the composition of the committee's shortlist. I was pretty certain that Rummel had never been shortlisted and succeeded in getting the committee's secretary to confirm that there was no evidence for it.[12] Evidently, Rummel had confused a news report that talked about a final list (i.e., a list of all nominations received before the deadline) with a

---

[12]Telephone conversation with Geir Lundestad, then Director of the Norwegian Nobel Institute, probably in 2005.

shortlist. Eventually, he stopped referring to his having been 'a finalist', following as he said 'advice from a colleague who I highly respect, is a friend who supports my research, and who is knowledgeable about the workings of the Nobel Committee'.[13]

A second friendly quarrel occurred when in 1995 I served as guest editor for a special issue on democracy and peace in the *European Journal of International Relations*. Rummel published an article on the monadic democratic peace—in fact his fifth-most-cited article. In a previous much longer and widely circulated version, Rummel had promoted the argument that if democracies don't fight each other, the world must necessarily become more peaceful as the number of democracies increases. Although the two referees had not picked up this point, I argued in my decision letter, as I have done elsewhere, that this was not necessarily the case (Gleditsch & Hegre, 1997). We went back and forth. I was prepared to concede the point, which was not central to the article, but not without a struggle. Therefore, I set out to explain my argument in some detail. Finally Rummel wrote back to me. 'Nils, you did it'.[14] I have always felt that scholars should not give up their cherished views too easily. For that reason, I valued Rummel's persistence, although some surely would call it stubbornness. Nevertheless I am happy to have influenced this article and perhaps, even if in minor way, contributed to its success.

Finally, one of the perks of being president of the International Studies Association is the power to award the Susan Strange award to the scholar 'whose singular intellect, assertiveness, and insight most challenge conventional wisdom and intellectual and organizational complacency in the international studies community'.[15] Nothing would have pleased me more than to give this award to Rudy when I served my term in ISA in 2009—but he had already received the award! In fact, he was the first, in 1999. I can think of no one more qualified in terms of challenging conventional wisdom and intellectual complacency.

1.6   A Final Assessment

Rudy Rummel was a many-faceted scholar. It was not difficult to find things that you could disagree with. But there was also much to admire. His scholarly productivity. His enormous contributions to data on democide. His consistent commitment to freedom and his marriage of research and policy advocacy. His pioneering example in making data and research procedures transparent. His early use of the internet and his comprehensive homepage, matched by few if any social scientists of his generation. Hopefully, this little volume will inspire some readers to go back to Rudy's own work, for inspiration and for contradiction, but above all to follow his lead in seeking new knowledge for a better world.

---

[13]See at: http://www.hawaii.edu/powerkills/NPP.FINALIST.HTM.
[14]Or something to that effect. I can no longer find the correspondence.
[15]See at: http://www.isanet.org/Programs/Awards/Susan-Strange.

References

Bond, Doug B (1988) The nature and meanings of nonviolent direct action—An exploratory study. *Journal of Peace Research* 25(1): 81–89.

Doyle, Michael W (1983) Kant, liberal legacies, and foreign affairs. *Philosophy & Public Affairs* 12(3): 205–235 & 12(4): 323–353.

Dulić, Tomislav (2004a) Tito's slaughterhouse: A critical analysis of Rummel's work on democide. *Journal of Peace Research* 41(1): 85–102.

Dulić, Tomislav (2004b) A reply to Rummel. *Journal of Peace Research* 41(1): 105–106.

Ensign, Margee M & Warren R Phillips (1980) *Political Science Reviewer* 10(1): 97–137.

Galtung, Johan (1964) A structural theory of aggression. *Journal of Peace Research* 2(2): 95–119.

Galtung, Johan (1989) The shape of things to be. Chapter 12 in Joseph Kruzel & James N Rosenau, eds. *Journeys through World Politics. Autobiographical reflections of thirty-four academic travelers.* Lexington, KY: Lexington Books (165–178).

Gartzke, Erik (2007) The capitalist peace. *American Journal of Political Science* 51(1): 166–191.

Gleditsch, Nils Petter & Håvard Hegre (1997) Peace and democracy: Three levels of analysis. *Journal of Conflict Resolution* 41(2): 283–310.

Haas, Michael (1965) Societal approaches to the study of war. *Journal of Peace Research* 2(4): 307–323.

Haas, Michael (2014) *Deconstructing the 'Democratic Peace': How a Research Agenda Boomeranged.* Los Angeles, CA: Publishing House for Scholars.

Harff, Barbara (1996) Review of Death by Government by RJ Rummel. *Journal of Interdisciplinary History* 27(1): 117–119.

Hazlewood, Leo (1976) An appraisal of the methodology and statistical practices used in the Dimensionality of Nations Project. In: Hoole & Zinnes, eds (176–195).

Hilton, Gordon (1973) *A Review of the Dimensionality of Nations Project.* Sage Professional Papers in International Studies 2(15). Beverly Hills, CA: Sage.

Hilton, Gordon (1976) An appraisal of the philosophy of science and research design involved in the Dimensionality of Nations Project. In: Hoole & Zinnes, eds (155–175).

Hoole, Francis W & Dina A Zinnes, eds. (1976) *Quantitative International Politics: An Appraisal.* New York: Praeger.

Maoz, Zeev & Bruce Russett (1993) Normative and structural causes of democratic peace, 1946–1986, *American Political Science Review* 87(3): 624–638.

Phillips, Warren R (1974) Where have all the theories gone? *World Politics* 26(2): 155–188.

Pinker, Steven (2011) *The Better Angels of Our Nature. The Decline of Violence in History and Its Causes.* New York: Penguin.

Ray, James Lee (1982) Understanding Rummel. *Journal of Conflict Resolution* 26(1): 161–187.

Ray, James Lee (1998) R. J. Rummel's Understanding Conflict and War: An overlooked classic? *Conflict Management and Peace Science* 16(2): 125–147.

Rummel, RJ (1966) The Dimensionality of Nations Project. In: Richard Merritt & Stein Rokkan, eds. *Comparing Nations. The Use of Quantitative Data in Cross-National Research.* New Haven, CT: Yale University Press (109–129).

Rummel, RJ (1970) *Applied Factor Analysis.* Evanston: Northwestern University Press.

Rummel, RJ (1971) Status field theory and international relations. *Report, Dimensionality of Nations Project* (50).

Rummel, RJ (1976a) *Peace Endangered: The Reality of Détente.* Beverly Hills, CA: Sage.

Rummel, RJ (1976b) The roots of faith. In: James N Rosenau, ed. *In Search of Global Patterns.* New York: Free Press (10–30).

Rummel, RJ (1976c) *Dimensions of Nations.* Beverly Hills, CA: Sage.

Rummel, RJ (1976d) The Dimensionality of Nations Project. In: Hoole & Zinnes, eds (149–154).

Rummel, RJ (1976e) Comments on the reviews of the Dimensionality of Nations Project. In: Hoole & Zinnes, eds (219–243).

Rummel, RJ (1976f) Bibliography of the Dimensionality of Nations Project. In: Hoole & Zinnes, eds (489–496).

Rummel, RJ (1976g) Understanding Conflict and War, vol. 2: *The Conflict Helix.* Beverly Hills, CA: Sage.

Rummel, RJ (1979) Understanding Conflict and War, vol. 4: *War, Power, Peace.* Beverly Hills, CA: Sage.

Rummel, RJ (1981) Understanding Conflict and War, vol. 5: *The Just Peace*. Beverly Hills, CA: Sage.

Rummel, RJ (1983a) Libertarianism and international violence. *Journal of Conflict Resolution* 27(1): 27–71.

Rummel, RJ (1983b) Wiberg's review essay on Rummel: A reply. *Journal of Peace Research* 20(3): 279–280.

Rummel, RJ (1985) Libertarian propositions on violence within and between nations: A test against published research results. *Journal of Conflict Resolution* 29(3): 419–455.

Rummel, RJ (1987a) On Vincent's view of freedom and international conflict. *International Studies Quarterly* 31(1): 113–117.

Rummel, RJ (1987b) This week's citation classic: Applied Factor Analysis. *Current Contents* (24): 16.

Rummel, RJ (1989) Roots of faith II. Chapter 22 in Joseph Kruzel & James N Rosenau, eds. *Journeys through World Politics. Autobiographical Reflections of Thirty-four Academic Travelers*. Lexington, KY: Lexington Books (311–328).

Rummel, RJ (1994) *Death by Government: Genocide and Mass Murder in the Twentieth Century*. NJ: Transaction.

Rummel, RJ (1997) *Power Kills. Democracy as a Method of Nonviolence*. New Brunswick, NJ: Transaction.

Rummel, RJ (2004a) One-thirteenth of a data point does not a generalization make: A Response to Dulić. *Journal of Peace Research* 41(1): 103–104.

Rummel, RJ (2004b) *War and Democide Never Again*. Never again series, vol. 1. Fort Lauderdale, FL: Llumina Press, http://www.hawaii.edu/powerkills/NH.HTM.

Rummel, RJ (2005) *Ending War, Democide, & Famine through Democratic Freedom*. Nonfiction supplement. Fort Lauderdale, FL: Llumina Press, http://www.hawaii.edu/powerkills/NA. SUPPLEMENT.PDF.

Rummel, RJ (2007) *The Blue Book of Freedom*. Nashville, TN: Cumberland House.

Rummel, RJ (2008) Freedom's Principles, http://www.hawaii.edu/powerkills/FP.PDF.

Russett, Bruce (1993) *Grasping the Democratic Peace: Principles for a Post-Cold War World*. Princeton, NJ: Princeton University Press.

Russett, Bruce & John R Oneal (2001) *Triangulating Peace: Democracy, Interdependence and International Organizations*. New York: Norton.

Swain, Geoffrey (1991) Review of Lethal Politics: Soviet Genocide and Mass Murder since 1917 by R. J. Rummel. *Slavonic and East European Review* 69(4): 765–766.

Van Atta, Richard H & Dale B Robertson (1976) An appraisal of the substantive findings of the Dimensionality of Nations Project. In: Hoole & Zinnes, eds. (196–218).

Vincent, Jack (1987a) Freedom and international conflict: Another look. *International Studies Quarterly* 31(1): 103–112.

Vincent, Jack (1987b) On Rummel's omnipresent theory. *International Studies Quarterly* 31(1): 119–126.

Wiberg, Håkan (1982) Review Essay: Rudolph J Rummel: Understanding Conflict and War, vols. 1–5. *Journal of Peace Research* 19(4): 369–386.

Rummel multi-tasking, with his oldest daughter Dawn. Photo from Dawn Akemi's photo collection

Chapter 2
Dad

Dawn Akemi

In 1980, I left Hawaii to attend American University in our nation's capital. My first class was Introduction to American Politics and the professor called out roll on the first day. After I'd heard my name and raised my hand, the professor paused and looked me over. 'Are you related to Professor Rudolph Rummel in Hawaii?' Stunned, I said, 'He's my father.' I had sat at the back of a horseshoe-shaped arrangement of tables and chairs, and everyone turned to look at me while the professor launched into an adoring speech about the value of my father's research and theories. I basked in a brief sensation of being the child of a celebrity.

It was something that needed to be reconciled with the man I knew: my goofy and spaced-out dad, whose brilliant intellect did not rise above the scatological joke or other off-color humor. He seemed so silly to me as a youngster that when I asked him what he did for a living and he said he was a scientist, I laughed at him and said, 'No you're not. Scientists are smart!'

Of course, he was smart, brilliant even. I was never a student of my father's and can't pretend to be an expert on his legacy. However, I was steeped in the knowledge he was accumulating, imparted to me in a family culture of near-constant intellectual discussions of current events and his research and views. He didn't believe in dumbing down information for children, and if I had the intellect to ask the question, then I deserved the full adult answer. This and much more I inherited from him as he leaves a legacy not only in his work but in his daughters.

He gave me his optimism and the general positive outlook of 'Don't assume a negative.' Looking back at the dark revelations from his statistical analysis of war

Dawn Akemi grew up in Hawaii, where the warm ocean breezes filled her spirit with an active imagination and deep wanderlust. She left at 18 to work her way through college in Washington, DC, and then pursued a variety of careers all around the United States. She worked as a Certified Public Accountant, a sales representative, a chef's apprentice, a server, an actor, a comedian, and a writer. A zest for travel has taken her as far as Europe, Australia, the Far East, and Canada. Her journeys and experiences gave her a love of storytelling which she believes to be the heartbeat of the soul. She lives in Los Angeles with her husband and two doggies. Stories inspired by her life are blogged at http://www.DawnAkemi.com. Email: dawnakemi@gmail.com.

© The Author(s) 2017
N.P. Gleditsch (ed.), *R.J. Rummel: An Assessment of His Many Contributions*,
SpringerBriefs on Pioneers in Science and Practice 37,
DOI 10.1007/978-3-319-54463-2_2

and death, it's a wonder how optimistic he could be. For many years, his study was decorated with the macabre, wallpapered with horrifying cover images of blood and strife, torn off of magazines. He called that inspiration.

He gave me a thirst for a worldview, a global understanding of the human condition, as opposed to something regional or cultural. I was given exposure to world politics, critical study, and philosophical thought for as long as I can remember. Both my parents put a primary emphasis on education and scrimped his university salary, living in the most expensive state in the Union, to send my sister and me to private schools.

He made me a seeker with an inquisitive mind, instilling the imperative to 'question authority', including his own. He taught me to stand up for what I believed, even if it went against norms or need (such as kissing up to a boss for job), or friendship. He was always available to discuss parenting rules and was willing to be persuaded to change them if I gave sufficient evidence as to their deficiencies. He was able to question his motives, go against the flow, and entertain new ideas. This took courage, a spirit for adventure in the mind.

He was a fantastic and very patient mentor and teacher. I was remedial in math, the only one in my family without a proclivity for numbers. Dad had to coach me in algebra and calculus and did so cheerfully. He also taught me chess. It didn't matter what he was working on. If I had an academic question or confusion, he would drop everything to provide an answer or assistance.

He believed in maintaining the physical body for a strong mind. My parents walked every day for exercise until his health failed him. Over the years, they became involved in two sports—bowling and tennis—and joined leagues so they could compete. He loved competition. All this he gave to me, especially a love for physical activity. He approached sports with the same methodology as his work, studying books and magazines to learn techniques and strategies, then applied his research and taught it to his family. Next, it was practice, practice, practice! A couple of months ago, I went bowling for the first time since I was a kid. I felt my father over my shoulder, whispering those long ago instructions in my ear, and my old bowling muscles came alive again under his tutelage. That evening, I felt very close to my Dad.

He encouraged me to 'Do what you love and the money will come.' This idealism has ruled my life as I followed my heart into a variety of experimental careers, encouraged by him at each risky turn: a Certified Public Accountant, a chef's apprentice, a salesman in food distribution, various positions in the restaurant industry, a working actor in theatre and the entertainment industry, and now a writer working on my first novel. Like my Dad, I had artistic yearnings, and have studied and worked in the arts for most my adult life. Dad was the first person to encourage my writing shortly after completing my college education, saying for years, even before I started, that I was a better writer than he. There was some fatherly pride in that statement, of course.

He gave his daughters the freedom to explore and discover who we were, and then to bring that person to life's challenges with full force. He fostered individuality in a world that often demands conformity. My father walked his talk by applying libertarian standards (his professed beliefs at the time, later to become even more extremely labeled as freedomism) to his parenting. This choice lent itself to a permissiveness during the liberal and experimental sixties and seventies that now seems surprising, even to me. He believed in letting us follow our instincts and trusted that we would learn and grow from the experiences. To protect us from that process with strict rules would interfere with our growth and may not have prevented us from doing what we wanted anyway. Only later did I discover this choice was absolutely at odds with his conservative Mid-western upbringing, and it sometimes kept him awake at night. My sister and I were beneficiaries of this heady freedom, as it was grounded in the rock-solid foundation of ethics and morality present in my father's work. He was no hypocrite.

This is important to say because I think my father can *look* like a hypocrite. His life's work was spent researching the causes of war. His last brag was that he gave the world a potential solution for world peace. He hated violence, yet supported the Vietnam War, both Iraq Wars, and a host of other US military actions abroad. He believed absolutely in our military buildup during the Cold War and continued to support it even after the Berlin Wall came crashing down. At various times, he's been accused of being a war hawk. There's still a framed cartoon from the 1970s on the wall in our family home where my Dad is lampooned as a war hawk, standing next to a colleague shown as a peacenik. He found it so absurd as to be funny and worth memorializing. He could be confusingly contradictory. I used to think of him as a fiscal Republican and a social Democrat, but then he really defied all labels.

I've always believed we're a complicated species in a complex universe we barely understand. Our world is organic, with messy boundaries and beautiful colors. It's impossible to impose upon it our black and white organizational grids without running into contradictions of their very purpose. I've never met someone with strong opinions who didn't sometimes look like a hypocrite. In that way, my father was like any other. He had layers of rationalizations for his hierarchy of beliefs. He would've called it all logical and scientific, but the rationalization of beliefs is a skin-deep penetration into my Dad. In truth, I think there are deeper reasons for his contradictions that lend insight but can never fully explain them. He understood gestalt and that 'You simply can't divorce … personal elements from your work.' In the end, he did manage to separate aspects of himself, very private personal elements that he didn't want to look at or reveal, proving we are all mysteries and contradictions unto ourselves.

My parents grew up in broken families filled with pain and sorrow, both suffering through trauma at a young age. My mother's formative years were indelibly scorched by the horrors of World War II in Japan, particularly the US firebombing of Tokyo. Her earliest memory is jumping into a ditch to avoid fire, her house aflame. Her father was a violent alcoholic who abandoned her and her mother when she was young. My father's parents were poor and irresponsible, and their relationship was equally conflict-ridden. He remembered being so hungry he searched for food crumbs in his pocket. Out of desperation, he ran away from home in his teens, living in the streets of slums.

Other than these publicly related facts, I don't know much more about either of my parents' upbringings. Their combined traumas left them defensive of too much psychotherapy, introspective analysis, and communication of feelings. Psychologists often need a psychologist, my Dad would often joke. So why bother? Neither forgave their past or parents, and both held onto a bitter privacy where they trusted few. They didn't heal their grief, as they didn't believe such a thing needed to be healed. Rather than try understanding these sorrows and transforming them into a compassionate inner understanding of themselves and the human condition, they clung to each other and stashed painful memories in a dark place, buried beneath intellect, where they hoped no one could see, including themselves. While compartmentalization is understandable, we can't isolate the shame or fear resulting from trauma, intern them in an emotional concentration camp, and expect them to stay confined without impacting society at large. Emotions remain alive, sometimes festering, often bleeding into the mind and heart with unintended consequences, or even psychosis. For my parents, those unexplored dark places created blocks and blind spots in how they reacted to and interpreted their environment.

My parents alienated others, including me, with their sense of righteousness and self-proclaimed 'hermit lifestyle'. Their laissez-faire, non-interfering approach to parenting, which gave me so much freedom as a child, could look like abandonment, especially once I left home as an adult. Attempts on my part to pierce the veil with questions as to the whys and wherefores of their behavior in order to connect more deeply to my father yielded gentle rebukes saying he 'didn't wish to psychologize' and 'wasn't laced with a disposition for introspective analysis'. My father's spirit for adventure came to a screeching halt at introspection. My mom was simply unapproachable on these matters. Their combined resistance was impenetrable.

In later adulthood, I presented the oft-used, very trite garden metaphor for relationships to my father: that gardens needed daily cultivation, such as watering or fertilization, and weeding or pesticides; gardens also needed space and time to grow, and could be given too much attention such as over-pruning or over-watering. I was searching for a language for how to bridge the ever-increasing distance between us that didn't directly demand he gaze at his navel. Before I could expound completely on the metaphor, my father stopped me and said, 'No, a relationship is like a landscape, to be viewed and appreciated from afar.' This stymied me and led to a five year silence between us where I withdrew to soothe my disappointment and, unconsciously, to test my father's mettle. How much distance did he need before he would inch closer? I never found out, because I broke silence when his health began to fail and accepted that such a question would never be answered.

In terms of the wider world, he loved studying politics but hated political playing. His journals revealed a man insecure in his ability to speak publicly and engage socially with aplomb, and so he kept himself private. Social expectations were an infringement into his chosen lifestyle and a threat to long-held protections of privacy. He kept a cerebral distance, a social and professional isolation, which also protected him from criticisms of his work. As with myself, his wider professional relationships were a landscape to be viewed and judged from afar. I've often wondered about possibilities if he had the openness to explore the mysteries of his own behavior beyond the scope of his focused numerical and scholarly analysis, to delve into self-awareness and introspection, to shine a light on his pain and personal sorrow, and to heal those dark festering spaces. He might have relinquished the need to separate himself, promoted his work with more skill, and achieved the wider recognition for his conclusions that he craved. Who knows what subtle layering and insights it could have brought to his analysis, or his ability to relate to his peers effectively?

My father's aversion to his inner world and anti-social tendencies may seem like splitting hairs in academia, but in the artistic world, it is the biggest inhibition to creative expression. He wanted to be an artist at one point and dabbled all his life. His painting was approached with the same methodical processes he gave his research: analyzing an image, breaking it down into a grid of smaller reproducible sections, and recreating the image with virtual photorealism and very little style. He left sitting out on his worktable an unfinished grid of a work-in-process of an old favorite picture of my sister and me. He also loved Photoshop, where he could play with filters, color, and line. He mocked abstract art and 'high-minded interpretations of pretentious art critics' in the world of fine art, especially when it came to modern and post-modern expression. He seemed to push away the subtleties of emotional and behavioral explorations inherent in such abstract work. His workman's approach to art wasn't a bad method, and he created some fine images. As in his life's work, he had much talent and skill to offer. However, his process was craftual and missed the bedrock of an artistic process which goes beyond the aesthetic to interpret an object or event, to look inward to see how it makes the artist feel and to imbue those feelings into the work. Art not only brings to life a subject, it expresses ideas and feelings. Our introspective emotions are what give art power. In return, art exorcises trauma by its release in expression. As intelligent as he was, I don't believe he metabolized this understanding, and it never came through in his art.

Dad considered the heart, with its often inconvenient emotions, to be an unreliable decision maker. 'Learn to control your emotions.' and 'Use your mind to control your body.' were two admonishments given to me and provided a strange contradiction to his ' … do what you love …' advice. It's true the heart alone cannot make all decisions. However, this is true of the mind as well. Both need to be consulted and both have valuable information to impart. Emotions need to be heard. Our bodies are more than a conveyance for our heads. Were he to have looked more deeply into his heart, into the dark recesses he had hidden away, he may not have been so quick to endorse policies of force against force. He may have found a more far-reaching conclusion. This too could've earned his work the recognition he craved.

All of this isn't to say my father was anything less than a great man, a great teacher, and a great father—those things don't demand great perfection. Nobody's perfect. American individualism purports that one discipline, or one person, can hold the key to saving the world from war, or rather, humanity from itself. I don't believe that. It's a very complex problem. My father died believing he had found a solution in the Democratic Peace Theory. Perhaps. What I do believe is he developed ideas whose time has not yet come, and he accumulated a mass of data that can be used to refine the analysis and solution. He laid a great foundation, and was a great benefit to humanity, a special man who overcame adversity and a tragic childhood to become a world-class scholar. He took that which was dark within him and used it to fuel light, as coal makes fire. He was my Dad, lucky for me, and I love him.

It's my hope that we're joining forces in this book to do more than simply eulogize and reminisce about my father. The authors of this volume, and others, are now charged with parsing and building upon his life's work. I present these personal recollections of him, both light and dark, in an effort to paint a more complete picture of the man behind the data and theories. If you imagine all knowledge as a big dark room, and that we all have flashlights to illuminate, teach, learn and grow from, then my Dad's light shone bright and wide. Yet he couldn't illuminate the whole room. No one can. He was but one man, beautifully imperfect, brilliant with the vitality of his unique life force. Progress in humanity is comprised of individuals building on the discoveries made by those who came before. It's a collective and cooperative synthesis of information and ideas, involving both the head and heart. This may eventually light up the room. The human journey isn't finished. My father's prime legacy, his research and analyses, will always help enlighten that which is dark.

Chapter 3
R.J. Rummel, Citizen Scholar: An Interview on the Occasion of His Retirement

Doug Bond

3.1 Introduction

Rudy Rummel's motivating passion—his lifelong aversion to conflict and violence—was eclipsed only by the fierce independence born of his experience as a homeless youth from a broken family.[1] His scholarship was characterized by his exceptionally rigorous and open-minded quest to test theoretical explanations with empirical data while explicating the associated assumptions and normative implications. His legacy, however, lives on in his example of a citizen scholar, whose commitment to take intellectual discussions beyond the academy into practice as he sought in everything he did to realize freedom and dignity with peace.

Doug Bond, b. 1954, Ph.D. in political science (University of Hawaii, 1985). He has held various appointments at Harvard since his arrival as a Visiting scholar in 1988 and is now a Lecturer in Extension and Research Advisor in International Relations at the Division of Continuing Education. He previously taught at Kyungnam University in Korea. In 1996 he founded a social science consulting company (Virtual Research Associates, Inc.) that conducts applied research and field training, and offers technical support for conflict early warning systems in Africa and elsewhere. Email: doug.bond@vranet.com.

[1]This interview was conducted in Honolulu, Hawaii on 4 September 1996 shortly after Rudy Rummel retired from teaching. As one of Rudy's relatively few Ph.D. students (less than twenty over thirty years of teaching), I sought to trace the origins and evolution of his values and views and to solicit his reflections on his interaction with the community of scholarship, and also on the lessons he learned in his life. In these excerpts from that interview, I draw mainly on Rudy's own words, editing only for readability. Parts of my introductory commentary were presented at the 46th Annual Convention of the International Studies Association, Honolulu, HI, in March 2005 at a panel celebrating Rudy's life work.

© The Author(s) 2017   23
N.P. Gleditsch (ed.), *R.J. Rummel: An Assessment of His Many Contributions*,
SpringerBriefs on Pioneers in Science and Practice 37,
DOI 10.1007/978-3-319-54463-2_3

3.2   A Premature Retirement from Teaching

Upon learning of Rudy's imminent retirement, I asked him if he was ill or if he was finally going to move back to the mainland, perhaps to join another university. He answered 'no' as he offered his explanation that began with a bit of personal history.

Rudy had hearing difficulties throughout most of his adult life. By the time I met him in 1979, his hearing loss was already evident and at some point he was fitted with a hearing aid device. In those days these devices were quite crude, so the echoing of the cinder block classrooms became an increasing challenge for him into the 1990s.

One day in the mid-1990s, while teaching in a large classroom, Rudy was leading a lecture-discussion using his usual Socratic method where he walked up and down the aisles interacting with the students. A student sitting at the far end of the classroom asked him a question and Rudy began to respond. However, even as Rudy responded he realized that he had not really heard the question. It was in that instant that Rudy made the decision to retire from teaching. If he could not hear well enough to interact with his students, he knew his teaching days were over.

By the end of that school year Rudy retired from teaching and began working full-time on his research, writing, and interaction via his evolving website and blogs with numerous colleagues and others. Most of these communications were done via email as Rudy increasingly avoided telephone conversations and minimized his travel.

3.3   A Scientist's Explicit Reference to Values

Rudy taught that science had three foundations: theory, data, and norms. He explained that all three operated together, and all were required for scientific inquiry. He also reminded his students that theory was always bounded, as was data. He emphasized the inherent limitations of operationalization and in the methods of measurement and he advocated the explication of all assumptions in any analysis.

Rudy was quite comfortable with the notion that all data are qualitative and some data are also quantitative. His view of scientific inquiry bridged the qualitative-quantitative chasm that has divided the academy for more than half a Century. His intellectual autobiography chapter (Rummel, 1976) was titled 'Roots of faith', to emphasize the importance he placed on motivating values and beliefs. Too often, Rudy lamented, the normative foundation of science went unexamined out of incompetence or ignorance, or was deliberately ignored due to a hidden agenda.

3.4   The Interview, Part I: An Aversion

Q: Could you clarify your initial aversion … was it to violence or to conflict?
RJR: It's both. I grew up in a very conflictual family. My parents were divorced at a very early age and as a young boy I remember arguments of one sort or another between them. It's conflict that I'm talking about here. I developed an aversion to people getting into arguments and fighting between people in what was called conflict of some sort, whether it's violent or nonviolent. Cussing at each other, for example, was a form of conflict which I developed a strong aversion to and the aversion comes out of my youth and my family, with parents who couldn't get along and argued constantly and subsequently got divorced with a devastating impact on me because at a young age I was on the street.

I quit high school because of that. When I was of legal age, I could, and did quit at 16. So I was on my own at a very young age which, incidentally, had a great impact on me as an academic and a student because having my family destroyed under me, being left alone to do what I could for money. I actually starved because I didn't have any food, and going through my pockets looking for bread crumbs to see if I could find something to eat, having to go fishing in Lake Erie to catch fish so I could go around to bars and try to sell it so I would have some money to buy something to eat.

Having had, in other words, to order my own life so that I could survive on the street when I became a student, I wasn't about to be pushed around by professors. So when I became an academic, I wasn't about to be pushed around by my fellow academics or to go along with the consensus simply because I wanted to get along. So my independent streak which has been noted comes out of that early experience which is always a part, it's a gestalt, the growing independence, the aversion to conflict, the desire to see accommodation between people and conflict while at the same time (in my mid-teens) I was learning how to get along in the world in a way that I could survive.

However, I was in a dead end. I was working as a common laborer in a variety of jobs that I hated. Again, I'm by myself, no family. I joined the army when I was 18. What else am I going to do, ok? I had dreams of being perhaps an equipment operator because no one around me completed high school and nobody around me had a college education. I didn't even conceive of a college education. So I went into the army and volunteered for Korea. I ended up in Japan in an engineering battalion.

Now that experience had two incredibly important effects on me. One of which I developed as a result of growing up during World War II, viewing the Japanese as buck-tooth, monkey-like, implacable, stoic, and violent—all of this from the war propaganda that I had assimilated as a very young boy. I get to Japan and I find the Japanese very much like I am. They could cry, they could love flowers, they could play with dogs. They had a full range of emotions, a full range of desires. And as a result of that I went through a cultural shock you might say. How come we made war against these people?

Now it's one thing if the Japanese are all that they were purported to be from the propaganda that I got during World War II, if they fit the stereotype that I learned … but they weren't. They were like you and me. It was a profound cultural shock. When I went to Japan in 1950 you could still see horrible wounds of war, and I became very anti-war. Why are we making war? We shouldn't make war on each other. Now, this is where the violent part of my aversion came, my aversion to the violence of war. What I saw in Japan. The aversion toward conflict came in with my family experience.

The second incredible impact was, by an act of God, I ended up in this engineering battalion in Tokyo which was making maps for the Korean War. They would get the data in from the planes doing the survey, then they would make the map immediately. Those maps would be sent out to divisions that needed them. I had no skills at the time. The reason I ended up in this battalion is because of how much I built up my earlier factory work to sound like it was great, so they put me down as an engineer.

In any case, the people around me had college degrees. I didn't even have a high school education. So I find myself with people with college degrees. Well, wait a minute, they are not so bright! Hey, I know more than some of these people. And I get back to the tremendous influence on my whole life in research. From this experience there percolated the idea of going to college. And then I read a book in Japan called *The Professor's Umbrella* (Mary Jane Ward, published in 1948), which was about the life of the professor and that was it. I was going to go to college. Not to be become a professor, as such at that time. But none-the-less, I'm going to go to college.

And so I studied while I was in Japan. I learned fractions, learned roots, and all that sort of stuff. Studied grammar, studied history and finally took the GRE exams for the high school equivalent diploma. I took those. I passed them and I had my high school equivalent diploma. When I got out of the army I applied for Ohio State University.

These are the circumstances that fueled my hatred of war and why war became the focus of my early research. I saw war as the worst kind of conflict, the worst kind of violence.

3.5   The Interview, Part II: An Affinity

Q: You have commented about science fiction. Please explain.
RJR: One more extraordinary influence on me that melted into everything else was science fiction. I was on my own. I didn't have money for movies. I didn't have a TV. I don't even recall if I had a radio. When I left home I went to work on a farm and in my spare time I read. I got interested in

science fiction books and I really got educated through them. I developed a fascination for science. I developed some knowledge of astronomy and other kinds of science and I developed a vocabulary.

That was over a six or seven year period. I read virtually everything that came out in science, virtually everything that I could get my hands on. I became, therefore, in love with science. And as a matter of fact, I felt that I could talk more knowledgably about science from what I learned from science fiction than could those with college degrees in the army that I talked to.

I was in my early teens when I was into science fiction. As a result of that, when I went out to college and eventually found out that I could focus on the study of war, what an amazing discovery that was. I had no prior knowledge of that. I was first going to major in physics and math, in large part because of the science fiction. I was going to go into rocket research. However, I also found myself reading social science stuff, especially on Asia. So I transferred to the University of Hawaii because I felt I could better study Asia in Hawaii. This interest of course was developed during my stay in Japan. I could speak Japanese conversationally.

I came here [to Hawaii] and had to choose a major. I was interested in Asian studies, but was advised to major in political science because I was told it would better prepare me for securing a job. I was persuaded by that. So I took political science as my major. And I found out soon enough that in the field of international relations I could study war. It was amazing. To me this was a blinding discovery in that I wanted to do something about war. I'd seen the horror of it in Japan and I thought that it was wrong for people to make war on each other. Here was a way to study it and do something about it. And so from then on, I focused on why people fight each other and what I could do about it.

One of the first courses that I took at Hawaii was Introduction to international relations and the text book had a chapter on war. I learned that war was a respectable sub-major, and thereby one could focus the study of war. My first term papers were related to war in one way or another like unilateral disarmament, why we should unilaterally disarm. I thought that if we didn't have arms, we wouldn't have war. So my first naïve term paper, I think, was to the effect that we should unilaterally disarm.

3.6   The Interview, Part III: Science as a Profession

Q: How did your aversion to conflict and war come to interact with your interest in science fiction?

RJR: Science was a method. The substantive topic was violence. Violence and war in particular, was the extreme form of conflict. When you have war, you have people massacred by plan, by states and therefore, it seemed to me in the hierarchy of conflict and violence, the worst is war. I didn't know anything about democide, except for the Jews.

My aversion to conflict began when I was a young boy because of my parents. My aversion to war, which I knew nothing really about until I got to Japan and saw what was going on, came later. I became quite anti-war, and I created problems for myself as a result. Orientation sessions in the Army were conducted for the troops. They explained to us why we were fighting the Korean War. A Lieutenant would give a reason and I would say can't the North Koreans give the same reason for fighting the war? I refused to salute the flag. I resisted these kinds of things because I thought nationalism was evil. Nationalism being one of the reasons we went to war.

So as a young boy, I went through this whole route. I was an absolute pacifist, absolutely anti-war and absolutely opposed to nationalism. I was also, to a certain extent, anti-American and a dedicated socialist. I was a left-wing, anti-war type when that wasn't a respectable thing. So, as you can imagine, I had all kinds of problems. I remained a Private first class throughout my career, except for the last months before I got out, they made me a Corporal.

3.7   The Interview, Part IV: Worse than War

Q: At what point did the cracks start appearing in this world view that perceived war as the greatest thing to be overcome?

RJR: That was gradual. My view on war became inconsistent with what I was beginning to understand about war. I wrote a paper logically detailing why unilateral disarmament would not work. The field of international relations at that time was not consistent with the pacifist view. I refer here to the idea of a balance of power, the idea of war as a way of settling what diplomacy cannot, the rationalization and justification of World War I and World War II.

As I began to study World War II, I could not see how a pacifist could justify allowing Hitler to conquer nations and kill people. Increasingly it seemed to me that World War II was a just war. Now if we have one just war, how can one say that all wars are bad? If we have one just war, how can one be an absolute pacifist? So I moved to the Christian position. I subscribed to the classical Catholic position on just war. Wars are evil, but if the evil that would occur if one were not to fight is greater than the evil of war, then one is justified in fighting.

Q: Can you articulate the standards that you applied to these issues?

RJR: It was just change. The values were already there and what happened was an accumulation of things that were inconsistent with what I thought was the empirical world to which the values apply. For example, my anti-war stance, my absolute war stance is based on the empirical assessment of the world, of history, of how people operate. I have these basic values and the question is always how to implement them and what I see as implementation inconsistent empirically and theoretically gets discarded and I grow to accept those that seem to be a better fit with the world.

Consequently I moved to accept the reality of nuclear weapons and their usefulness as a deterrent, something that horrified pacifists. I was not horrified. Now, one can argue with me that my view was wrong. We can talk about that. But an assumption that because I was in favor of nuclear weapons as a deterrent and somebody else isn't, my values are all crooked, I think is wrong. It's not a matter of values, it's a matter of practice and where the practice is inconsistent with the world, then I think the practice has got to be changed.

3.8 The Interview, Part V: A Liberal Education

Q: You have characterized the early 1970s as the era of your liberal education. Could you elaborate?

RJR: Oh yes, that was quite an education. I took a leave from my research management responsibilities. I continued to teach. I came in one day a week for my class and I'd do the necessary decision-making on the project. I was able to take off day after day reading the basic books in the social sciences. That was a very liberal education, something I never got before to that depth. And that influenced me in two basic ways. One, my philosophy changed from positivism, I'd say almost rigid positivism, to a kind of mushy mixture of positive science on the one hand and intuition and imagination on the other. Where I saw the virtue I felt there was a virtue now to intuitive insights, to imagination, to traditional scholarship as well as science. One melds these together as a conductor melds orchestra together in producing a scientific work. That was quite a change. It's still science. But now I relaxed and terms of my definition of science to include imagination and intuition.

The second influence was that I changed from socialism to libertarianism. I was a democratic socialist, not a state socialist, not a marxist, I was never a marxist. I never believed in authoritarian socialism but nonetheless I was really a socialist, at least for a while. The reason I moved on, is that I grew to see through all the reading that I had done that socialism was unsustainable, as a doctrine or a theory an unsustainable practice.

Q: So at this point, your evolution did not include any fundamental shift in your perspective on war?

RJR: My position with respect to war did not change until I did my first work on democide and that was in the early 1980s. I began to think about war differently because some of the things I came across were crazy. Like the Soviet Gulag, for example, and China under Mao. Of course I knew about what Hitler had done in Yugoslavia, Romania, Hungary, and so on but I hadn't yet put together how many people were being killed.

By 1984 or so I finished what I thought were conclusive studies on the relationship between freedom and violence. I decided to deal with these facts and do a pilot study on genocide and mass murder. I found that in this century about 110 million people had been killed in cold blood. That was an incomplete study. It was done in something like six months. On that basis I went to the US Institute of Peace for funding to do a comprehensive study. That started right away in 1986. This work was completed in 1995, and out of it came five books.

My conclusion was that is war is not the worst evil: four times more people are killed in cold blood by governments than die at war between governments. That was a shock. That shook me. I had a lifetime devotion to doing something about war because I thought it was the worst evil, the worst violence and I discover that democide is the worst violence.

Equally important was that the solution for war that I found is the same solution to democide. The solution of freedom was consistent with my values, the empirical evidence and theory.

3.9   The Interview, Part VI: Theory Informed, Data-driven Research

Q: Is there anything else that influenced the evolution of your aversion to conflict and violence?

RJR: No. It is unusual how focused I've been in a field where you see colleagues jump all over in terms of their research without apparently an underlying theme. For me, there was only one reason for the research that I did. I wanted to help solve the problem of conflict and violence, particularly war. Keep in mind that my single mindedness did not mean that I focused on war to the exclusion of other kinds of violence. I saw war as a part of a continuum and that to understand war one had to understand other forms of related violence such as war within societies, civil war, revolutions, and also to understand the associated conflict. So I did a tremendous amount of research in psychology and sociology. In my *Understanding Conflict and War* volumes I tried to articulate a theory that helps us better understand conflict as a continuum from conflict through violence which is the conflict helix.

I have placed in our discussion so far an inordinate amount of emphasis on the empirical side. To me, data have to be interpreted. How do you interpret data? You have to have a theory. What is a theory? It is a formal system that can be disproven. How do you disprove it? You disprove it through by trying to make it fit the empirical world, the data. Thus, what has to come first is theory. Once you have the theory, then you collect the data to disprove it. In other words, the theory has to be falsifiable à la Popper.

I saw the Dimensionality of Nations (DON) project as a way of helping to generate the theory. One of the intellectually satisfying events of my life happened at the black board in my study at home, at Yale. I had been doing the factor analysis of nations and attributes. I had conducted both monadic and dyadic analysis of nations and these were two separate things within the DON project. That bothered me. There was a tension there that had to be resolved. And it all came together when working on the black board. Mathematically I found that I could take the distances in the space of attributes as forces in the field of dyads so that the two fields were joined. The distances between the dyads became the forces.

Now, this field theory was not dissimilar from the notion of distance in sociology or from Quincy Wright's use of distance in his book on war. What was new to me was to be able to mathematically link these two spaces. From then on the DON project became one of articulating this theory, collecting the data, testing it out because the theory was that the distances in the one space would predict to conflict and war, the behavior of nations.

3.10   The Interview, Part VII: Lessons Learned

Q: Do you have any lessons that you would like to offer, any admonitions?
RJR: Don't assume a negative. Because so many students say don't do this or don't do that, and I say try to do it rather than assume you can't.

Also, I suggest prioritizing family. One's family is essential and why I think it is so necessary to talk about gestalt. At the core of my life are my wife Grace and our two daughters. I suppose one reason for this is because my own family was destroyed, that is my mother and father. I was not going to let this happen to my daughters. Family integrity and family first remains a dominant element in my life. You can't divorce these familial elements from one's philosophy of science, no more than one can separate data from theory from norms. All are amorphously integrated.

International relations and political science are still pre-professional. There is not a strong tradition of reviewing research, for example. That people will do research without reviewing what has already been done is an incredibly weak facet of our profession.

Finally, there is a very strong intolerance of different ideas and different approaches. So many people in the field have firm beliefs that their approach is the only one or their substantive conclusions are the only right conclusions. They then attack people personally when their research findings differ. There is an absolutism in one's own conclusions and research that ought not to be part of the scholarly or scientific field. We must all accept that we could be wrong. We probably are in many respects and let's find out how.

Reference

Rummel, RJ (1976) The roots of faith. In: James N Rosenau (ed.) *In Search of Global Patterns.* New York: Free Press, 10–30.

Chapter 4
Rummel as a Great Teacher

Sang-Woo Rhee

4.1 The Great Teacher

Professor R.J. Rummel passed away in the spring of 2014. The ashes of his body are now floating on the waves of the beautiful Kaneohe Bay he had loved so much, but his soul and teaching will live on in the minds of his students. For them he will forever remain a 'Great Teacher.'

A Great Teacher himself should be a 'perfect intellectual,' since he is supposed to train mature intellectual leaders of the community. A Great Teacher should be a man of integrity who inspires others through his words and deeds. A Great Teacher should be a role model for his disciples.

Rudy Rummel devoted his whole life to the study of war and conflict. Enhancing peace had been his life-long academic goal. Throughout his whole academic career, he concentrated his teaching and research on peace studies. Based on empirical analysis of various cases of democide, the mass murder of citizens by their own government, he concluded that psychopathic totalitarian ideologies such as Nazism, Leninism, Maoism, and Japanese militarism are the real enemies of peace. From these studies, he derived a simple but very strong thesis: 'freedom fosters peace'. His libertarian peace theory was developed in support of this belief. His magnum opus, *Understanding Conflict and War* is the main output of his endeavor.

Rummel then launched a vigorous public campaign to spread his message. He wrote a series of novels, *Never Again*, as well as *The Blue Book of Freedom* to propagate his belief to the men on the street. His students were moved not only by his academic sincerity but also by his deeds. Rummel was a real Great Teacher who led his students to try to emulate his life style.

Rhee Sang-Woo, b. 1938, Ph.D. in Political Science, University of Hawaii, 1971; Associate Director, DON Project, 1971–73; Professor of Political Science, Kyung Hee University and Sogang University, 1973–2003; President of Korean Association of International Studies, 1991; Chairman of Presidential Commission of the 21st Century, 1987–94; President, Hallym University, 2003–07; and President, *New Asia Research Institute* (NARI), 1993–present; Email: swrhee38@gmail.com.

© The Author(s) 2017
N.P. Gleditsch (ed.), *R.J. Rummel: An Assessment of His Many Contributions*,
SpringerBriefs on Pioneers in Science and Practice 37,
DOI 10.1007/978-3-319-54463-2_4

A Great Teacher should also be a good scholar and maintain academic prominence. To maintain his academic excellence, Rummel educated himself constantly in order to continue as a positive role model. He read enthusiastically until the day he drew his last breath. He read widely, even exploring books written by ancient Chinese sages as well as Western classics. Based on his readings of works by Chinese scholars such as Confucius and Mencius, he held intensive discussion sessions on neo-confucian political doctrines with his Korean students. Aside from his own field of political science, his reading covered a wide range of areas from mathematics, philosophy, and aesthetics to psychology and sociology. *Understanding Conflict and War* elegantly demonstrates the breadth of his knowledge. He wrote a total of twenty books, and it is difficult to believe they were written by a single person. With his guidance and advice a new generation of students were groomed into mature scholars.

4.2   Rummel's Korean Students

During Rummel's tenure at the University of Hawaii, for ten years, the East-West Center annually brought in two Korean students for graduate training. Among these students, more than half chose Rummel as their academic advisor. They felt intellectually comfortable with Rummel and were attracted by his *Weltanschauung* that was congenial with oriental academic thinking.

Traditional Oriental philosophy is based on the belief that the Universe evolves following its own laws of change. We call it Heavenly Reason (*tien-li*). Since human beings are partial elements of the Universe, they should abide inter-personal ethical codes (*ren-tao*) derived from the *tien-li*. Political doctrines for communal governance (*chi-tao*) then should reflect the *ren-tao*. Rummel's firm belief in 'Man in Nature' contrasts with the prevailing Western assumption of 'Man versus Nature' and was easily accepted by his Korean students. According to the standard thinking in the oriental culture, a man's identity is determined by his combined relations with other people and things. Inter-personal relation is not the calculated distance between men. Rather, the relations determine the identity of the man. These ways of thinking fit with Rummel's concept of 'field'. 'A nation's attribute distances from other nations in A-space will determine its behavioral pattern in B-space'. This is the core argument in Rummels Field Theory, and one that his Korean students could easily accept. These shared perspectives led Rummel's Korean disciples to accept his theoretical arguments easily.

Professor Rummel started his teaching career at Indiana University and then taught at Yale University for two years. In 1966 he moved to University of Hawaii, where he taught for 30 years until he chose early retirement in 1995. During his tenure at University of Hawaii he served as the academic advisor for twelve Korean Ph.D. students, more than half of the total number of Ph.D. candidates he advised. Of the twelve Korean students, six wrote their dissertations under Rummel's guidance. Most of them returned to Korea and assumed professorship in various

Korean universities and actively promoted Rummel's work to their colleagues and students. In the Korean academic community they were known as the 'Rummel School.' They introduced Rummel's theories, beliefs, and arguments in their own monographs and textbooks. In addition to their academic activities, Rummel's Korean disciples also made a major contribution to the Korean government's foreign policy development. For example, Dr. Chang-yoon Choi, who taught at the Korean Military Academy, was later recruited by President Roh Tae-Woo to serve as Minister of Culture and Information. Dr. Yong-ok Park who greatly contributed to development of Rummel's Field Theory Model II while he worked as a research assistant for the DON Project, taught at the Korean Defense University and later served as Deputy Minister of National Defense. Dr. Jong-yul Lee, another DON research assistant, was elected to the National Assembly and served President Chun Doo-Hwan as Chief Secretary of Political Affairs and Minister of Political Affairs. Another DON assistant, Sang-Jin Choi, joined the Ministry of Foreign Affairs and later served as Ambassador to Finland. Dr. Young-Sun Song, the youngest Ph.D. student in Rummel's Korean brigade, worked as chief policy analyst at the Korean Institute of Defense Analyses and was later elected as a Member of the National Assembly. I myself, after thirty-year long teaching career at Sogang University, worked for the ROK government as Chairman of Policy Advisory Committee in the Ministry of Foreign Affairs and Ministry of Unification. I also served as Chairman of the Presidential Commission of the 21st Century and as Chairman of the Military Reform Committee of the Ministry of National Defense.

Rummel's academic achievements are perhaps even better known in Korea than in the United States, since he has been more broadly introduced in Korean academic journals and textbooks than in any other country. His Korean students share his critical thinking, his democratic values, and his political outlook, as well as his attitude toward academic research. Through these Korean students, Rummel's philosophy and ideology of libertarian peace is widely spread among the Korean intellectuals.

4.3 My Own Work with Rummel

It was in 1967 that I first met Professor Rummel at University of Hawaii. I was awarded an East-West Center scholarship sponsored by the US State Department, which enabled me to pursue graduate studies at University of Hawaii. Until I earned my doctorate in 1971, Professor Rummel was my academic advisor. I completed my dissertation, 'Communist China's Foreign Behavior: An Application of Field Theory Model II,' under his guidance.

For two years thereafter, from 1971 to 1973, I assisted Rummel in managing the Dimensionality of Nations (DON) Project, as its Associate Director. I was also deeply involved in projects dealing with issues related to conflict and war among nations as well as peace-related theories, which were his core research subjects throughout his academic career.

I returned home to Korea in 1973. To disseminate what I learned from Rummel, I I invited Rummel to Korea in 1978 to teach a two-week special summer class for graduate students from universities all over the country. I also arranged for his book *In the Minds of Men* to be published by Sogang University Press. This book has been used as a textbook by many universities in Korea. Then I translated and published his two books, *Democide* and *The Blue Book of Freedom* in Korea. I also collected some of his writings, including his autobiographical account 'Roots of Faith' along with some of my own essays in a book. This volume was published in Korean as *Rummel's Libertarian Peace Theory*. Unfortunately, my laziness prevented me from doing more to disseminate this work and others that highlight his great achievements—which I still regret today.

Since I returned to Korea in 1973, until three years before his death, I went to visit Rummel and Grace in Hawaii at least once a year. Whenever we met, even after I became a retired professor in my mid-seventies, he gave me a 'special lecture' on new research trends in political science and kept me abreast of the progress of his own research projects. These lectures easily lasted a few hours. I was clearly his lifelong student.

4.4   Freedom and Dignity

Rummel's love for all of humanity, transcending ideology, race and social status, were limitless. His students including myself were deeply moved by his love for humanity. While fire is the source of light, so love is the source of peace. Love signifies respect for the dignity of fellow human beings. Only those who enjoy freedom can respect the dignity of others. This led Rummel to conclude that 'freedom makes and fosters peace'. He had a firm belief in the need for an order of community whereby all human beings could enjoy freedom and happiness regardless of their social status, 'liberated from the willfulness of others'. He thought peace was an order whereby all human beings could co-exist with mutual respect. This philosophy became deeply imbued into the minds of his students. His determination to contribute to establishing an order of peace launched him on a lifelong academic career devoted to the study of peace, and his students tried to emulate his life.

Rummel sincerely listened to all theories and arguments made by others that were put forth, whether or not he agreed to them. Without obstinacy, he listened to what others contended with an open mind. He was perhaps one of the best-read scholars. Listening to diverse opinions, he carefully selected useful ones and accommodated them in his theoretical frame. He always sought to extricate himself from bias, and such an open scholarly attitude moved his students.

Rummel was not a pedantic scholar. He was more interested in down-to-earth 'human life' than in academic theories. To him, academic research had no significance in itself; it had significance only when it provided the wisdom needed to improve realities or to promote the welfare of humanity. For instance, he searched through historical facts to locate instances of mass murders by dictators (democide) to show the world how such events devastated the lives of ordinary individuals. Most of his later academic efforts were geared toward identifying instances of democide in order to develop a system to prevent it. His series of novels, *Never Again*, is an outcome of such efforts. Rummel's positive academic approach deeply influenced his students, who followed in his footsteps and adopted empirical approaches to research.

4.5 Rudy in Space

Professor Rummel quietly passed away in the spring of 2014. As dictated in his will, his body was cremated and the ashes were scattered in Kaneohe Bay. Although his body has disappeared, I do believe that his mind will be wandering in space forever. I also believe his love will live on in the minds of his students, for whom he will forever remain a Great Teacher.

I often have dreams in which I see Rudy flying in space with a bright smile, holding hands of his wife Grace. I do miss him and Grace.

Rummel's Work Published in Korea

Rummel, RJ (1984) *In The Minds of Men*. Seoul: Sogang University Press.
Rumel, Rudolp J [RJ Rummel] (2004) *Demosaid* [Democide]. Seoul: Guiparang (in Korean).
Rumel, RJ [RJ Rummel] (2006) *Bulubuk: Jayujuei Cheongseo* [The Blue Book of Freedom]. Seoul: Guiparang (in Korean).
I Sang U [Sang-Woo Rhee] (2002) *Rumel-eui Jayujueui Pyunghwa-Iron* [Rummel's Libertarian Peace Theory]. Seoul: Oruem (in Korean).

Chapter 5
Contextualizing Rummel's Field Theory

Richard W. Chadwick

5.1 A Genealogical Preface

I first met Rudy[1] in 1962 when I was an incoming graduate student at Northwestern University. Harold Guetzkow was then the principal investigator of the Dimensionality of Nations (DON) Project, Harold appointed Rudy as his project supervisor while Rudy was working on his dissertation. I was recruited by Harold to work on the project as a data collector and statistical analyst. We worked well together because of the rigor with which Rudy pursued his work on the DON Project, an integral part of his thesis research. My job was initially to run basic statistical analyses on published data put into tables by other graduate students. I also collected data on conflict behavior within and between states for the period 1955–57 by content analyzing microfilmed *New York Times* (*NYT*) indexes. Rudy and Harold developed an initial typology of conflict, defining threats, accusations, protests, ultimatums, anti-government and anti-foreign demonstrations, numbers killed in domestic and in foreign violence, and other variables. We modified these definitions many times because the initial definitions were incompatible with the terminology used by the *NYT* Index. At first, we found that inter-coder reliability correlations between three *NYT* data coders (including me) using the same sources and years with the same definitions, was almost exactly zero. At the same time,

---

Richard W. Chadwick, b. 1939, Ph.D. in political science (Northwestern University, 1966). He worked on the DON Project 1962–63 at Northwestern under R.J. Rummel and again part time while an associate professor at the University of Hawaii from 1968 to the close of the project in 1975. He remained a colleague of Rummel in the Department of Political Science until the latter's retirement. Email: chadwick@hawaii.edu.

[1]I use Rudolph J. Rummel's nickname. To honor the friendship we had in the first decade we knew each other, 1962–72. We parted ways at the University of Hawaii long after the DON Project finished, over our politics and related matters, the details of which would probably shed far more heat than light if they were not long since forgotten.

© The Authors(s) 2017
N.P. Gleditsch (ed.), *R.J. Rummel: An Assessment of His Many Contributions*,
SpringerBriefs on Pioneers in Science and Practice 37,
DOI 10.1007/978-3-319-54463-2_5

Rudy independently collected data from the *NYT* itself, which provided much greater detail. The reliability problems were eventually resolved using a refined coding procedure (Rummel, 1966a).

In the course of these labors Rudy and I, often with Harold, had many extended and lively discussions about the meaning of what we were doing. Rudy was a Korean War veteran and in the middle of his pioneering dissertation research and Harold had a long professional history in psychology. When they spoke about their concerns, fears, and hopes, I, barely 22 years old with no similar experience, listened and probed. Out of such conversations, I formed the impression that we did not know enough as scientists, nor obviously did politicians, to prevent catastrophes such as wars, even potentially nuclear war.[2] Secondly, it was possible to learn more that might help to avoid war by studying social, political, and economic systems. And finally, quantitative modeling with the data we were collecting, might serve to structure the environment in laboratory-based human interactions designed to simulate foreign policy decision-making. In turn, this might further our knowledge of decision-making sufficiently to offer some progress towards reducing the likelihood of war. The urgency of this need for knowledge was widely recognized, and was at the core of Harold's creation of the Inter-Nation Simulation (INS) and the DON Project. INS had been set up to simulate foreign policy decision-making environments and DON was created to collect data to test hypotheses that would emerge from the INS work as well as to improve the quality of INS experiments. The intent was, as I understood it, that INS and DON would work together synergistically, the research output of each becoming input to the other over time. When Harold turned over the DON project to Rudy, he also closed INS and began the Simulated International Processes (SIP) project, which in time turned to all-computer simulation despite Guetzkow's initial preference for man-computer simulation. Though on a much smaller scale, the hoped-for INS-DON synergy was very much in the spirit of Wright's (1957) plea for a 'world intelligence center' to develop and disseminate knowledge aimed at reducing the likelihood of a global nuclear holocaust.

5.2   Field Theory Genealogy: Take-off Traces

The latent actor/agent-environment sketched above was a key component to field theory frameworks as well as constructivist thinking a generation later (Onuf, 1989) and quite distinct from the 'inherited traits' and Pavlovian and Skinnerian conditioning literature. I am not implying that their orientation was fully constructivist, only that the thinking of the many researchers who earned their MAs and Ph.D.s on these two projects had a common orientation towards decision-making and leadership which recognized that decision-makers and their environments were in large measure defined by the beliefs, attitudes, and situational orientations of participants.

---

[2]For a fuller discussion of this point, see Chadwick (2011).

In the classic S-O-R model, there was now substance not only in the 'O' but in the '-O-', the dashed lines representing communication in its symbolic and semantic fullness. As Richardson (1960: 12) put it, 'Critic: Can you predict the date at which the next war will break out? Author: No, of course not. The equations are merely a description of what people would do if they did not stop to think.'

One can see in this simple dialog with an imagined critic the latent field theory and constructivist insights, and also the need for the careful ontological synthesis done by Onuf, Wendt, and others two generations later. With this focus, Rudy was quite sensitive to social science theories and methods that might offer some pointers to make progress in the direction of more volition-oriented theory. It was in this learning process that Rudy introduced me to Quincy Wright's *The Study of International Relations*. In particular, he introduced me to Wright's review and interpretation of the general field theory approach to theory development (Wright, 1955: 524ff). Wright (1955: 546) introduces his field theory formulation with 'six capabilities and six value dimensions' ..., 'the rapidity and direction of movement of each depending in considerable measure upon the relation of its four structural levels. This cannot, of course, be represented visually in three-dimensional space, but imagination may picture a twelve-dimensional semi-opaque cheese, within which maggots crawl around, the larger ones representing states with the government at the head and the people at the tail.'

Wright did not take the representation further to develop a quantitative theory of international relations. He apparently got the idea of representing the movements of states as vectors in an n-dimensional space of countries' attributes from his brother, Sewall Wright, a geneticist and developer of path analysis. Jack Sawyer introduced Rudy to the basics of factor analysis, the technique used in the DON Project to uncover patterns in relations between variables. As I recall, some 236 variables were collected across 82 countries but because of insufficient data fewer were actually used. In the process I learned about factor analysis from him. I had an opportunity to return the favor after Rudy left first for Indiana University and then Yale, where Betty Bockelman assisted him in much the same manner. We were concerned with how to compare factors in analyses of different data sets with the same variables. Wandering through Northwestern's library my eye caught a book in the psychology section written by Ahmavaara & Markkanen (1958), which solved precisely the same analytic problem, though the substance was different (comparing the brains of alcoholics and non-alcoholics on various cognitive dimensions). The trick was to treat the factor loadings as ordinary variables and do multiple regressions of each factor's loading from one data set on the factor loading matrix of the other data set.

5.3 Systems Thinking

Systems thinking was then a relatively new paradigm for understanding the nature of creative change in beliefs, technology, and behavior of large aggregates of people. It starts with the assumption that there is continuous interplay between individuals and their environments complicated by the fact that individuals are a large part of each other's environment. From a paradigmatic perspective field theories are a type of systems theory that searches for causal explanations for individual interactions or events not in prior events or environmental circumstances, but in the purposive behavior of individuals shaped by their collective beliefs, perceptions, and experience of what is real, what is possible, and what is desirable. Understanding human behavior and communication in large aggregates over time is not something for which we humans have good natural perceptions, not to mention methods of organizing perception into data recordings, and even less explaining such systematic observations with theory. For example, Sawyer & Levine (1966: esp. 730f) applied factor analysis to cultural characteristics and concluded that comparative economic efficiency of types of social and political organization, rather than geographic cultural diffusion, accounts for similarities and differences among different cultural groups. Incomplete as it is, their work represents a very high level of grounded theory generalization about large scale human social systems, undetectable by individuals within those systems unless they have a prior appreciation for their system. A generation later, Inglehart & Welzel (2005) reach a similar conclusion, that economic development influences value change in increasingly democratic ways. For decades, these and similar results have pointed to the need to use dynamic factor analysis in foreign policy studies. Thus, over-time relationships can be perceived between changes in historical contexts, values, political policy judgments, and cultural changes related to economic and political development. Unfortunately, as Ricci (1984), Zegart (2015), and others have pointed out, the gaps between academics, operational policy analysts, and philosophers remain as abysmal as ever. We are still mired in historical institutionalism, path analysis, and social network analysis, or even neural net analysis, none of which enable us to see the forest for the trees, that is, the nature of human systems dynamics.

5.4 Field Theories

Field theory in the social sciences has an underlying system approach or paradigm, but it did not begin that way. 'Field theory' began its use as a term to describe models of magnetic and gravitational fields. By analogy, people are embedded in fields that attract or repulse them, not in the sense of electrical energy force fields but in Lewin's sense of culturally conditioned linguistic and conceptual environments that induce their psychological and behavioral predispositions. 'Fields' exist as individual and collective memories, motives, expectations, goals, and purposes distributed over a geographical region and fluctuating over time as people interact. The way Rudy put it much later, 'We are a dynamic field of needs, attitudes, sentiments, emotions, expectations, and perceptions; a subjective field within which the world is given a unique interpretation; a perspective through which reality is transformed.' (Rummel, 1976b, Sect. 2.1.) To use 'analogy as a source of knowledge' (Lorenz, 1974), consider computers. You cannot tell how people will behave unless you know how they are 'programmed,' what they are prepared for or 'need' for input, how they are being used, what is presumed to be available for output, and what decisions are made which creatively regulate that output. The 'political system' concept in the work of Easton (1953) fits this model, yet Easton himself, to my knowledge, did not take the next step to a 'field' framework.

Early development of field theory in the social sciences begins with psychology, chiefly in the work of Lewin (1939). In his framework, individuals (and groups) are conceived of as goal-seeking life forms in environments which, over time, induce learning. Environments are perceived as opportunities and obstructions to goal attainment, motivating people to adapt their behavior. The goals themselves vary as basic needs at the biological level are adequately met.[3]

All these ideas constituted my own 'little field' as I tried to understand the purpose of the DON Project and what my mentors were about. As I recall, Rudy began his thinking about fields with Wright's idea of states propelled by interests and power in an n-dimensional space defined by their attributes, and Lewin's idea of people interacting in fields constituted by their personalities. Over the next four or so decades, Rudy made their insights for understanding international conflict quantitatively and systematically researchable, at least in principle, and applicable to Guetzkow's and his concern with preventing war.

Lewin sketched his theory as an equation, B = F(P,E). Behavior B is a function of the life space of an individual, the personality P and environment E (Fig. 5.1). Here, the irregular sections represent an 'intellectual geography' or life space, that is, events or situations through which a person travels over time and which influence the person P moving from some origin O towards a desired goal G. Both the person and the environment are in flux, thus different people at different times experience different situations. Each person (or group) may well constitute one of those irregular shapes in the graph—each shape representing their 'field' of beliefs and predispositions, as each pursues their own goals in interaction with P. Although Rudy takes exception to this graphical representation, at the end of his critical review of the literature, he notes that he is in substantial agreement with Lewin's equation.[4]

Further, consider one of Rummel's concluding graphs (Fig. 5.2). As I see it, this is clearly a more detailed rendering of one of Lewin's irregular shapes, some details applying Maslow's concept of basic needs.[5] Thus, Rudy is integrating a variety of theories and, as such, makes an original contribution to at least one type of field theory.

Rudy represented his field theory of international politics by this simple equation,

$$X_{ij} = \alpha j_1 f_1() + \alpha j_2 f_2() + \cdots + \alpha j_p f_p() + U_{ij}$$

---

[3]While researchers and theorists are cognizant of environmental, anthropological, and genetic perspectives, the feedback dynamics at various levels of analysis are not explicitly modeled in this field theory approach.

[4]See at: http://www.hawaii.edu/powerkills/DPF.CHAP3.HTM (search for Lewin). However, Burnes & Cooke (2013), building on Rudy's critique, find the graphic representation superior to the mathematical modeling attempted by Lewin himself.

[5]Rudy discusses Maslow's theory of basic needs extensively in Chap. 21; see at: http://www.hawaii.edu//powerkills/DPF.CHAP21.HTM.

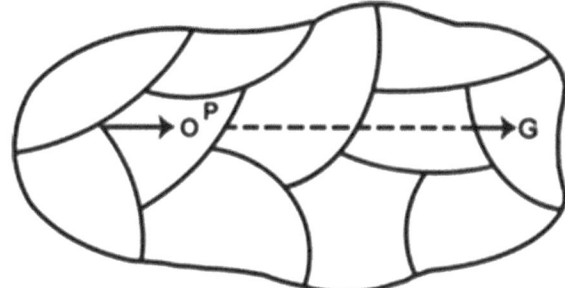

Fig. 5.1 Graphical rendering of Lewin's field concept. *Source* https://commons.wikimedia.org/wiki/File:Lewin%27s_field_theory_2.png

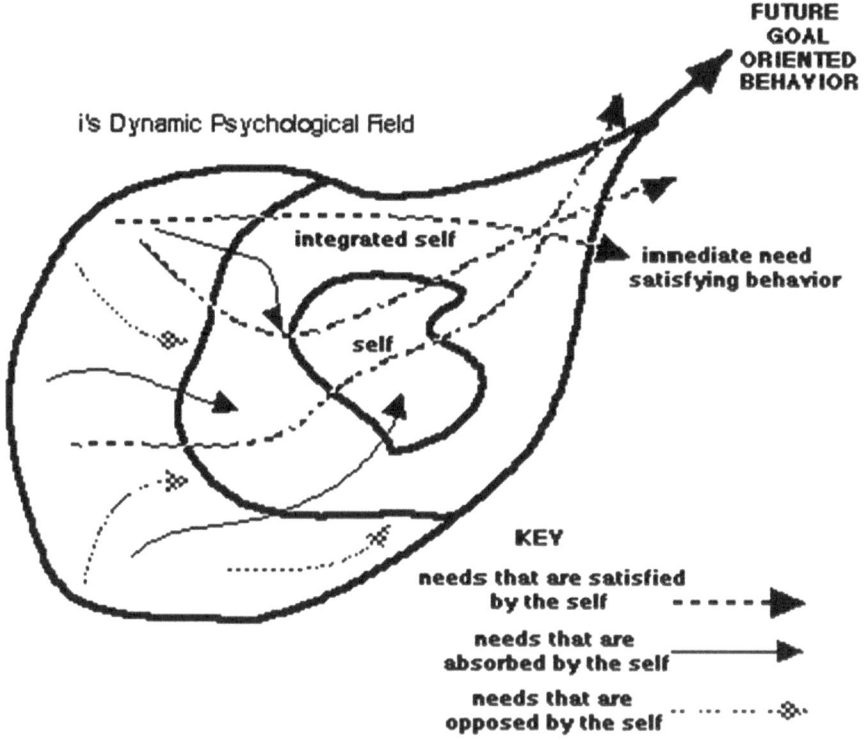

Fig. 5.2 Rummel's sketch of the dynamic psychological field. *Source* Rummel (1975), Fig. 28.2; see also Chap. 3

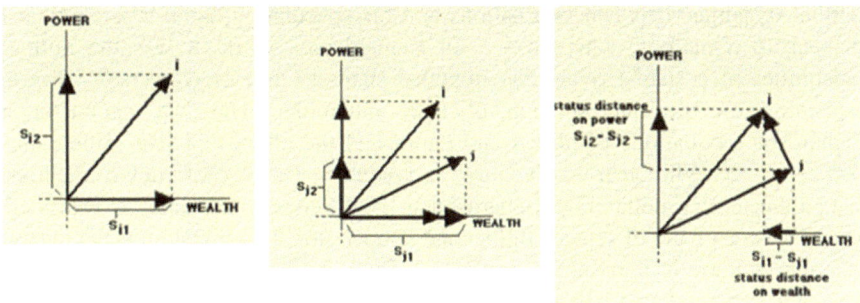

Fig. 5.3 Rummel's power and wealth distances and vectors. *Source* Rummel (1975), Fig. 17a–c. Models based on this framework can become quite elaborate; for instance, see http://www.hawaii. edu/powerkills/WPP.FIG7.1.GIF applying it to totalitarianism

where X_{ij} is a 'behavioral manifestation' j taken by an actor i, the α's are parameters regarding the behavioral manifestation, the functions $f_{1...p}()$ in the equation are intentionally left blank to represent the myriad latent functions composing a personality and an environment, and U_{ij} represents the person's uniqueness.[6]

To connect to traditional international politics research, consider Fig. 5.3. Here power and wealth are represented as vectors motivating states as decision-making units to pursue survival through increasing power and wealth. So far, this is fairly standard realist theory, expressed in a field-theoretic language.

Several key ideas in Rudy's field theory make his perspective unique. The first is 'distance',[7] usually conceived in a multidimensional space of differences between states' attributes, and typically related to estimates of power differentials. I write 'usually,' because although the vast majority of his work related differences in states' attributes to differences in their behavior (as did Wright, 1955), some of his earlier work (Rummel, 1966b) used a variety of functions, multiplying attributes for instance, with significant results. In discussions with him, I inquired as to why he abandoned all but differences in attributes to produce differences in behavior; the only answer I recall is that alternatives just were not elegant. Simplicity and beauty are hallmarks of great theories, true enough, but then there is also evidence.

Another key characteristic of Rudy's field theory is the construction of data tables on pairs of states (dyads). Tables with dyads in rows and attributes or attribute differences in columns are hallmarks of his theory. But quite apart from the role such tables played in his field theory, that very format was a stroke of creative genius, independent of whether the dyadic contents were conceptualized as 'distances' or some other function of attributes I had not seen a prior use of data in that format. The closest, even in principle, was Richardson's (1960) differential equations modeling

---

[6]This equation is found in Rummel (1975), Chap. 11 and is, I think, fairly representative of the generality of other equations in other chapters on related topics.

[7]The 'distance' concept is explicated throughout Rudy's writing, but see Rummel (1976b). Rummel (1966b) experimented with a departure from 'distance' as a key concept.

conflict dynamics between two nations and his speculation about extending such analysis to n nations, where n > 2. In Richardson's work, it was the military capabilities of a state's rivals that impelled states to arm or conversely, disarm, depending on the interpretation of their intentions. The fear parameter in Richardson's equations amplified and dampened the effect of power differentials between states. While fear was included as a parameter in his best-known equations, that parameter was defined by Richardson as the difference ('distance' in Rummel's terms) between pairs of states' conflict and cooperation. (Cooperation was seen as a function of trade in the Kantian tradition.) Thus, it was not simple differences in attributes that produced behavioral differences. Rather, attribute differences evaluated by differences in conflict and cooperation levels between them, create variable levels of fear that in turn produce behavior (arming or disarming). One might infer that mathematical 'field theory' has a longer history than conventionally assumed, since Richardson first published his work as early as 1919.

The power and wealth vectors in Fig. 5.2 could be roughly measured with DON data or similar collections, to calculate differences between states, but 'rough' also implies—for the obvious reasons of validity and reliability—low associations with behavioral data. Van Atta & Rummel (1970) used 1963 international relations and state attribute data to test the differences cause behavior hypothesis. They found no relationship (no variance in behavior explained by differences alone); however when they controlled for certain 'uniqueness' of states, they found about half the variance in behavior explained. Aside from the technical questions posed by using the method of canonical factor analysis (the first canonical factor accounted for about half the variance in the 'space' defined by the first three behavioral dimensions), the difficulties of operationalizing a field theory are formidable. Consider that the 'field' contains the psychological dimension, the beliefs goals, values, worldview, and so on, none of which were made operational with data. Given these handicaps, the results, though disappointing, might have been expected.

Rudy wrote a critical overview of other field theory approaches,[8] which focuses on the research being insufficiently cross-disciplinary in theory construction and integration, on being insufficiently grounded in data, and on being insufficiently sophisticated in mathematical formulation. These criticisms, valid as they are, are fairly representative of scientific enterprises in general and Rudy's would seem to be no exception: The equations and graphical illustrations shown above are not much different in detail, his data difficult to come by and analyze, and his integration of his theory with other disciplines incomplete. By the late 1970s, Rudy himself shifted from further development of this framework to immersing himself in traditional international relations and cognate fields' literature mostly devoid of mathematical representation and rigorous logical deductive formats.[9]

---

[8]See http://www.hawaii.edu/powerkills/DPF.TAB6.1.GIF for a tabular summary and Rummel (1975), Chap. 6 for the detailed review.

[9]Rummel (1976a) was drafted much earlier, and contains a self–analysis of why he moved to non–quantitative literature for inspiration.

To stop at this point in evaluating field theory in general or his in particular would be a disservice to both, for one needs to understand the larger context of this shift from quantitative, empirically grounded research to the traditional library research of scholars. The DON Project research agenda required substantial funding and the principal supplier was ARPA. This funding ceased by 1975. However, research of a quantitative nature into international politics continued inside the intelligence community. For instance, this is where Stuart Bremer's GLOBUS Project ended up, after starting at the Berlin Science Center thanks to Karl Deutsch. It had created a massive database and embodied a variety of theories about the international behavior of states. Similarly, Mihajlo Mesarovic's WIM computer simulation, originally supported by the Club of Rome, morphed into the Pentagon's Globesight model and Aristotle database.[10] For several decades following Guetzkow, relatively large-scale quantitative international relations projects were well funded, and as uses for them were found they lost their public funding and drifted into the world of intelligence. To think that field theory and its parallel constructions failed to develop would, I suspect, be a mistake.

5.5 Parallel Constructions

Burnes & Cook (2013) have written an extensive review of 'field theory' research by that name. A broader framework, however, placing field theory in a larger social science context, would be highly desirable. Only a few generations ago, about all that existed of 'political science' was what we now call leadership theory, public policy and administration, and political philosophy. Psychology was dominated by the psychoanalysis schools inspired by Freud and behavior conditioning theories of Pavlov and Skinner. Crowd psychology, especially mob psychology (Le Bon) hinted at a crude form of field theory. But so far as I can see presently, it was the insight of Adam Smith and the dynamic 'invisible hand' of the market place (the idea that the behavior of individuals and communities in interaction had a dynamic of their own that needed to be understood as distinct from individual psychology or crowd dynamics), that ushered in a third 'level of analysis,' the system level. Today, of course, there is wide acceptance of the insights by Singer (1961) and others' that at least three analytic levels (individual, organizational or bureaucratic, and systemic) are needed in international relations theory, each with their own structures and functions. But even today, there is no systematic effort to integrate them into a multi-level theory, not to mention to follow the work of Richardson to examine longer term multi-nation dynamics. In this context of inchoate theory development, Rudy's field theory transcends earlier efforts in relative clarity and comprehensiveness.

---

[10]For a short time in 1990 I acted as a 'scientific adviser' for the Pentagon to evaluate Globesight and Aristotle at DRMEC (Defense Resources Management Education Center) at the request of its then Director, Robert von Pagenhardt, in the Naval Postgraduate School.

Rudy did not extend his formal field theory research to other problems than those of understanding the behavior of states, preferring more expressive modalities, art and literature appreciation, painting, and writing novels to express his deeply held humanitarian values such as the avoidance of nuclear war. However, using Rudy's field theory equations and his more philosophical discussions of their implications, one could imagine reinterpreting theories that are more partial in scope, for example, operationalizing an historical institutionalism framework with dynamic factor analysis, applied to historical trends in the satisfaction of basic needs, trends in the organizational structure of corporations, governments and empires, and so on. One could imagine reinterpreting social network analysis projects in terms of field theory 'distances' between 'nodes' (people, groups, ...). Similarly, in business management, Deming (1982, 1993), who became well known for his systems approach to understanding the dynamics of corporate-consumer relations, assumed that we all live in systems (organized relations) which determine our average behavior, that all systems decay and require intentional effort to be maintained and reinvented as technology changes. His insights can easily be incorporated into field theory. And as long as field theory equations are understood to be describing the behavioral dynamics of human interaction at different levels, even constructivist interpretations in terms of 'rule making' (Onuf, 1989) can find a place. Rules and rule changing can be understood to be both the outcome of adapting to the patterns described by field equations and the independent (exogenous) sources of new patterns in 'differences' described by field equations. Such speculation is a far cry from imaging states as Wright did, as maggots with states as heads and people as tails, vaguely sensing each other and moving by instinct in a 12-dimensional green cheese. But we still have a long way to go.

5.6   Implications and Possible Applications

Sooner or later, a generation of better mathematically equipped political scientists will take advantage of the power of computers and big data to test theories of human decision-making at multiple levels, and find ways to integrate such models into our political and social cultures through education.[11] That is, if we do not disintegrate first in some 'spasm' nuclear war, nuclear winter, man-made pandemic, or some such. I am reminded in that regard of an archeological dig in Petra, Jordan, of a culture that excelled at sandstone carving, building thereby a city of over 30,000 people by some estimates, in the middle of a desert. They had learned to harness water resources which gave them an economic advantage throughout the region. They were apparently destroyed by a series of earthquakes that obliterated their dams and wiped out the entire infrastructure, a catastrophe from which they never

---

[11]Cattell (1972) expressed this viewpoint quite eloquently and referenced Rummel as one of many pioneers in this path.

recovered. From a field theory perspective, it was the interaction of the environment with the culture and the motivational landscape of the people in it and other cultures that related to it, that created the disaster, hence could have been avoided.

For me the question arises, do we have equivalent 'fault lines' in our thinking and our cultural edifices? There is a long list of current dangers to our civilization, developed by a number of scholars.[12] Do we have the time to develop this field theoretic perspective, as I am sure Rudy would hope, given his focus on freedom and democracy, to identify such fault lines and educate ourselves at all levels so that we can in fact empower ourselves as a species, if not a culture, to survive them?

I've come full circle from Guetzkow's and Rudy's concern with the catastrophic potential for nuclear war, via Cattell's review of the infant steps of political science to address such issues and the details of Rudy's field theory developments following the efforts of Wright and Lewin, to a number of complementary developments in systems theory of which field theory is a part. I also noted the non-mathematical developments in constructivist thinking which complement field theory rather than compete with it, if field theory is understood to describe the environment within which people learn to make decisions and in turn change their environments. As with the human actors in Guetzkow's Simulated International Processes Project, perhaps the least developed aspect of field theory is precisely that noted by Rudy when he hypothesized that 'We are a dynamic field of needs, attitudes, sentiments, emotions, expectations, and perceptions; a subjective field within which the world is given a unique interpretation; a perspective through which reality is transformed.' We have mapped much of the environment of human decision-making, but very little in decision-making in comparison with the work ahead. Field theory is still in its infancy, but current researchers like Inglehart and Schwartz are teaching it to walk.[13]

References

Ahmavaara, Yrjö & Touko Markkanen (1958) *The Unified Factor Model*. Helsinki: Finnish Foundation for Alcohol Studies & Stockholm: Almqvist & Wiksell.

Burnes, Bernard & Bill Cooke (2013) Kurt Lewin's field theory: A review and re-evaluation. *International Journal of Management Reviews* 15(4): 408–425.

Cattell, Raymond B (1972) *A New Morality from Science: Beyondism*. Elmsford, NY: Pergamon.

Chadwick, Richard W (2011) My mentored relationship with Harold Guetzkow. *Simulation & Gaming* 42(3): 308–313.

Chadwick, Richard W (2014) Fraud and deceit, or a failure of American political and social sciences: Towards a theory about the impact of banking on the rise and fall of civilizations. *International Relations and Diplomacy* 2(10): 639–654.

Deming, W Edwards (1982) *Out of the Crisis*. Cambridge, MA: MIT Press.

---

[12]For a modest effort of my own at coming to grips with one of them, see Chadwick (2014).

[13]See Inglehart & Welzel (2005, 2010) and Schwartz (1994) and Dobewall & Strack (2014) for a comparison.

Deming, W Edwards (1993) *The New Economics for Industry, Government, Education.* Cambridge MA: Center for Advanced Engineering Study, MIT.

Dobewall, Henrik & Micha Strack (2014) Relationship of Inglehart's and Schwartz's value dimensions revisited. *International Journal of Psychology* 49(4): 240–248.

Easton, David (1953) *The Political System: An Enquiry into the State of Political Science.* New York: Knopf.

Inglehart, Ronald & Christian Welzel (2005) *Modernization, Cultural Change, and Democracy: the Human Development Sequence.* New York: Cambridge University Press.

Inglehart, Ronald & Christian Welzel (2010) *Changing Mass Priorities: the Link between Modernization and Democracy.* New York: Cambridge University Press.

Lewin, Kurt (1939) Field theory and experiment in social psychology. *American Journal of Sociology* 44(6): 868–896.

Lorenz, Konrad Z (1974) Analogy as a source of knowledge. *Science* 185(4147): 229–234, available on-line at https://www.nobelprize.org/nobel_prizes/medicine/laureates/1973/lorenz-lecture.html.

Onuf, Nicholas Greenwood (1989) *World of Our Making: Rules and Rule in Social Theory and International Relations.* Columbia SC: University of South Carolina Press.

Ricci, David (1984) *The Tragedy of Political Science: Politics, Scholarship and Democracy.* New Haven, CT: Yale University Press.

Richardson, Lewis Fry (1960) *Arms and Insecurity.* Pittsburgh, PA: Boxwood.

Rummel, Rudolph J (1966a) A foreign conflict behavior code sheet. *World Politics* 18(2): 283–296.

Rummel, RJ (1966b) A social field theory of foreign conflict behavior. *Peace Research Society, Papers* 4: 131–150.

Rummel, RJ (1975) Understanding Conflict and War. Vol. 1: *The Dynamic Psychological Field.* Beverly Hills, CA: Sage.

Rummel, RJ (1976a) The Roots of Faith, in: James N Rosenau (ed.) *In Search of Global Patterns.* New York: Free Press, 10-30.

Rummel, RJ (1976b) Understanding Conflict and War: Vol. 2: *The Conflict Helix.* Beverly Hills, CA: Sage.

Sawyer, Jack & Robert A Levine (1966) Cultural dimensions: A factor analysis of the World Ethnographic Sample. *American Anthropologist* 68(3): 708–731.

Schwartz, Shalom H (1994) Are there universal aspects in the structure and contents of human-values? *Journal of Social Issues* 50(4): 19–45.

Singer, J David (1961) The level-of-analysis problem in international relations. *World Politics* 14(1): 77–92.

Van Atta, Richard & RJ Rummel (1970) Testing field theory on the 1963 behavior space of nations. *Dimensionality of Nations Project Report* (43), http://www.dtic.mil/dtic/tr/fulltext/u2/710989.pdf.

Wright, Quincy (1955) *The Study of International Relations.* New York: Appleton-Century-Crofts.

Wright, Quincy (1957) Project for a world intelligence center and the value for conflict resolution of a general discipline of international relations. *Conflict Resolution* 1(1): 315–325.

Zegart, Amy B (2015) Cloaks, daggers, and ivory towers: Why academics don't study US intelligence. In: Loch K Johnson (ed.) *Essentials of Strategic Intelligence.* Santa Barbara, CA: Praeger, 31–48.

Chapter 6
R.J. Rummel, Nuclear Superiority, and the Limits of Détente

Matthew Kroenig and Bardia Rahmani

6.1 Introduction

Amid the intense security competition of the Cold War, the decade-long détente between the United States and Soviet Union stands out to many as a moment of pragmatic cooperation among rivals. The 1970s saw, among other developments, the adoption of arms control treaties such as SALT I and II, scientific collaboration between astronauts and cosmonauts, and the expanding of trade ties between Washington and Moscow. Bookended by the crises of the 1960s and the proxy wars of the 1980s, détente is the chapter of the Cold War in which peaceful coexistence seemed closest at hand. 'Détente is peace', wrote political scientist R.J. Rummel, 'Who in his right mind could speak out against peace?' (Rummel, 1976: 22).

In *Peace Endangered: The Reality of Détente* (1976), Rummel does just that. Tipping his hat to its intuitive appeal, Rummel nonetheless dismisses détente as faith, not sound policy. By conflating arms control and cooperative interaction with a durable peace, détente, in his view, weakened the West relative to the USSR and, in so doing, made war more, not less, likely. Détente, Rummel argues, is a road paved with good intentions and bad assumptions. And it is a road that forks off in one of two directions: nuclear war or unconditional Western surrender. 'This is the only choice', Rummel writes, 'unless we understand the dilemma and act to avoid it' (Rummel, 1976: 19).

Nearly forty years later, it might be tempting for us to dismiss Rummel's arguments as analysis distorted by Cold War paranoia. After all, history has proven Rummel wrong on many counts: America did not surrender to the Soviet Union;

Matthew Kroenig, b. 1977, Ph.D. in political science (University of California at Berkeley, 2007) is an Associate Professor in the Department of Government and School of Foreign Service at Georgetown University; Email: matthew.kroenig@georgetown.edu.

Bardia Rahmani, b. 1993, is an honors student in the School of Foreign Service at Georgetown University; Email: brahmani12@gmail.com.

© The Author(s) 2017   51
N.P. Gleditsch (ed.), *R.J. Rummel: An Assessment of His Many Contributions*,
SpringerBriefs on Pioneers in Science and Practice 37,
DOI 10.1007/978-3-319-54463-2_6

Moscow was neither resistant to the logic of mutual assured destruction nor as reckless as Rummel feared; and there is now substantial evidence that cooperative transactions can, in fact, lay the groundwork for peace among nations.

Nevertheless, it would be a mistake to conclude that Rummel's analysis of the nuclear arms race does not have important implications for those of us wrestling with similar issues today. Despite several predictions that missed their mark, Rummel's work sheds light on a number of fundamental scholarly debates, including those related to the nature of power in international politics, arms control, and nuclear deterrence. Moreover, many of his arguments seem evergreen in the light of a renewed Russian nuclear threat in contemporary Europe. Rummel's work, therefore, offers enduring lessons not only for international relations scholars, but also for policymakers attempting to minimize the enduring danger of nuclear annihilation.

6.2   Rummel's Arguments

Rummel identifies the logic of détente as stemming from two major assumptions. The first is that increased transactions between nations will result in greater harmony in their relations. Since cooperative transactions, such as trade, treaties, and conferences, tend to build trust, they establish a framework for nonviolent conflict resolution. Rummel calls this assumption *Détente 1*.

The second assumption, which Rummel calls *Détente 2*, is that we can reduce conflict between nations through arms control measures. Henry Kissinger described strategic arms reductions as 'the single most important component of our policy toward the Soviet Union' (Rummel, 1976: 24). According to Rummel, Kissinger viewed conflict as a product of the unbridled growth of national power and, therefore, Kissinger believed that limitations on military capabilities help states to cultivate peaceful relations and avoid war.

Rummel takes aim at both assumptions, beginning with Détente 1. From a theoretical standpoint, Rummel objects to the dichotomy between conflict and cooperation. A more apt bifurcation, Rummel argues, would be between isolation and interaction—conflict and cooperation being two different manifestations of the latter. Rummel offers the analogy of two individuals marooned on an island. The castaways can either (a) not interact or (b) combine efforts to find food and shelter. If they opt to do the latter, conflicts will naturally arise over any number of issues— for example, the appropriate distribution of resources. Conflict serves to rebalance the power dynamic between the castaways, creating a new status quo in which cooperation is also possible. Rummel's point here is not that interaction will necessarily increase conflict, but that we should also not expect cooperation to necessarily engender peace.

The numbers, Rummel argues, bear out his conclusion. Dividing cooperation into four categories (cooperative transactions, student flows, joint membership in international organizations, and trade), and analyzing thousands of bilateral interactions between nations, including those between the United States and Soviet Union, Rummel finds cooperative interaction and conflict to be uncorrelated. He does find that conflict begets conflict. For example, he finds that military action and anti-foreign demonstrations are correlated. But insofar as the central premise of Détente 1 is concerned, cooperative transactions reduce neither the frequency nor the scope of inter-state conflict.

Rummel begins his critique of Détente 2, the notion that arms control reduces conflict, with an examination of the nature of power. Rummel observes that capability, or military strength, is 'often mistaken for power's essence' (Rummel, 1976: 49). A more holistic notion of power should incorporate two additional elements: interests, or national attention toward a goal, and credibility, which Rummel defines as collective will—a nation's ability to transform attention into action. Power is the sum of capability, interests, and credibility. If one of these three variables flags, power decreases, and if any of the variables is zero, a nation will be effectively impotent.

This leads to Rummel's criticism of Détente 2: proponents of détente dangerously conflate capability with power. Détente, Rummel writes, 'considers neither interests nor credibility, but focuses on military strength as the variable most related to conflict.' By attempting to lock in the US-Soviet balance of power through 'essentially equivalent' reductions in military capability, détente has the practical effect of unbalancing the bilateral relationship. This is because, according to Rummel, the Soviet Union has more invested in winning the Cold War; its geographical location and ideological commitments imbue it with greater resolve. Pointing to America's withdrawal from Vietnam, its removal of military bases from South Korea, and what he considered its self-sabotage in the nuclear arms race, Rummel paints a picture of a nation in retreat. Meanwhile, the USSR's invasion of Czechoslovakia, its infusion of aid to the North Vietnamese and the marxists in Angola, and its support to the Arab states during the Yom Kippur War, demonstrate its 'superordinate interest in defeating the West' (Rummel, 1976: 50). Because US nuclear superiority serves to offset the Soviet Union's advantages in terms of interest and credibility, arms control disproportionately harms the United States.

Rummel backs his assertions with statistical analysis, finding that '… neither parity nor superiority in military capability is associated with bilateral peace' (Rummel, 1976: 55). This seems to fit with Rummel's multifaceted understanding of power. So long as interest and credibility factor into the overall balance of power, quantitative evaluations of military capability will fail to tell the whole story.

After addressing the internal logic of détente, Rummel turns his attention to its practical effects. Rummel accuses Soviet leaders of engaging in bad faith, and American leaders of acting on blind faith. According to Rummel, while Washington views détente as a means of diffusing the security dilemma, Moscow sees it as 'a tactical policy change to permit the Soviet bloc to establish its superiority in the next 12–15 years' (Rummel, 1976: 29). This mismatch in expectations, therefore, puts the West in a position of unknowingly ceding global hegemony to the Communist bloc.

Comparing a range of US and Soviet military indicators (and acknowledging that Soviet figures can only be estimated), Rummel calculates that far from maintaining 'essential equivalence', the détente-era arms control agreements ceded significant advantages to Moscow. He found that, from cruisers to cruise missiles, Moscow bested Washington on 40 out of 48 measures of military strength (see Fig. 6.1). Further, in the eight categories in which the United States led the USSR, it generally did so by a narrow margin, whereas the Soviet Union maintained robust

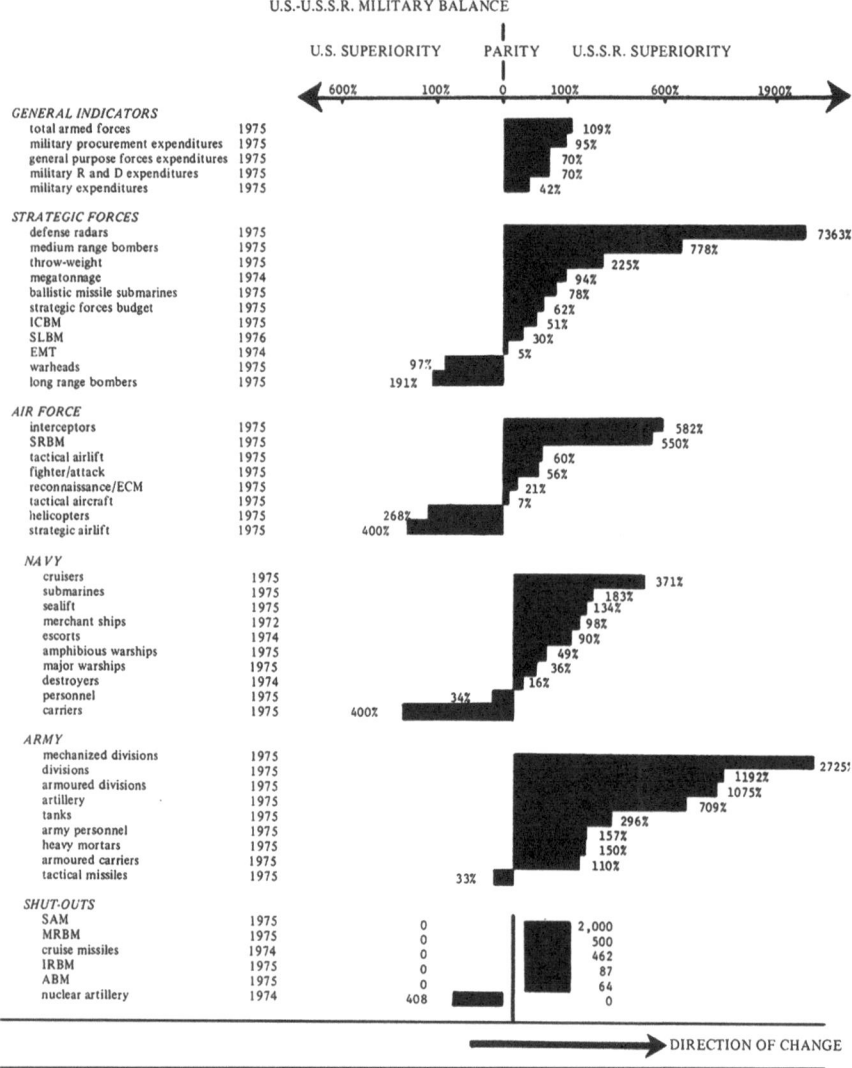

Fig. 6.1 Rummel's estimate of the US-USSR balance of military power. *Source* Rummel (1976: 60–61). Reprinted by permission of the publisher

leads. 'The stark picture that emerges,' Rummel writes (1976: 133), 'is of an overall Soviet superiority that will continue to grow.'

Crucially, while the two sides arguably maintained a rough parity at the strategic nuclear level, Rummel saw America's capabilities along the spectrum of conflict as an invitation to war rather than a bulwark against it.

This is because, according to Rummel, nuclear deterrence rests on three pillars. First, each side must have sufficient strategic force to survive a surprise attack and retaliate with unacceptable damage on the attacker; neither side must be allowed to develop a first-strike capability. Second, each side must have adequate military power to meet diverse threats at all rungs of the nuclear escalation ladder, including tactical nuclear weapons. If there is a clear weakness for an opponent to exploit, this will encourage an attack and could force the actor with gaps in its capabilities to fall back on its strategic nuclear weapons. Third, each side must have robust conventional capabilities, which prevents them from resorting to nuclear options in the first place. If an actor can respond with conventional force, conflict might be contained. But if it must instead resort to tactical nuclear systems, this will make it easier for an exchange to escalate to the level of massive retaliation.

Rummel's view was that, under détente, the United States lost its conventional and tactical nuclear edge, and as a result was forced to rely too heavily on its strategic nuclear warheads. US weakness at the conventional and tactical nuclear level made it more likely that a conventional clash would snowball into all-out nuclear war. On the other hand, if Washington refrained from escalating to avoid this outcome, it would essentially cede victory to the USSR. Hence Rummel's central thesis: détente, by creating a power imbalance, forces an inevitable decision between American surrender and nuclear war. Furthermore, because Moscow recognizes Washington's dilemma, it may be motivated to initiate armed conflict in the first place.

In the final section of *Peace Endangered,* Rummel addresses the state of NATO's strategic nuclear arsenal. Given the Soviet drive toward military superiority, could it be possible for the USSR to one day gain strategic nuclear superiority, depriving the West of one of its few remaining advantages? Could this superiority grow to such an extent that the Soviets even achieve a first strike capability?

In answering this question, Rummel distinguishes between a preclusive first strike and a dominant one. A preclusive first strike deals only with the technical ability of the Soviet Union to completely destroy the American strategic arsenal, eliminating its retaliatory capacity. A dominant first strike focuses on a nation's will to retaliate. Rummel argued that even if the Soviets were technically unable to wipe out the US offensive strategic force, they might still achieve a dominant first strike if they could dissuade Washington from retaliating.

According to Rummel's calculations, the Soviets 'will soon have a preclusive first strike, if not by 1977 [one year after the book's publication], at least by 1981' (Rummel, 1976: 137).

Even if estimates of Soviet strategic capability are overblown, however, Rummel argues that the Soviets may already have achieved a dominant first strike. He asks the reader to imagine a surprise attack that takes out the majority of US land-based strategic forces, but leaves its sea-based forces and population centers intact. Moscow then issues an ultimatum: retaliate against our strategic forces, and we will destroy a city; retaliate against our population centers, and we will launch an attack that will kill roughly 100 million Americans. No matter how Washington responds, Moscow would be better positioned for any escalation. In such a scenario, Rummel argues, the choice would once again be between suicide and surrender—no choice at all. Rummel writes: 'Our weapons were meant to deter aggression. If deterrence fails, would a president still press the button? Of course not.' (Rummel, 1976: 141).

By pursuing a strategy built upon the shaky pillars of cooperation, disarmament, and misplaced empathy, Rummel concluded that American policymakers put the United States at a strategic disadvantage. He argued that détente must be abandoned, but objected to critics who claimed that this put the superpowers on a path to war. He writes,

Throughout history, peace has been maintained by clear purposes, military power, and the will to use it. … When a nation's purposes become confused, its strength eroded, or its credibility questioned, aggression against it is encouraged, and is likely to occur (Rummel, 1976: 149).

According to Rummel, therefore, the solution is clear. The West must regain its military edge, demonstrate its willingness to use force, and reaffirm its commitment to winning the Cold War. In Rummel's view, it is military weakness, not military power, which is the principal cause of conflict.

6.3   The Legacy of Peace Endangered

Evaluating *Peace Endangered* is a challenging task. On the one hand, Rummel's prediction that the Soviet Union would achieve a first-strike capability, and that it might exploit this military imbalance to launch a nuclear sneak attack, never came to pass. Not only did the US emerge victorious from the Cold War, it did so despite a persistent nuclear deficit. By the conclusion of the Cold War in 1989, the Soviet Union's total nuclear stockpile outstripped that of the United States by some 13,000 warheads (Natural Resources Defense Council, 2006). Nevertheless, the internal weakness of the Soviet system and its disproportionate military spending placed the country on an unsustainable course—a fact that does not emerge in Rummel's analysis of national capability.

Rummel's criticism of Détente 1 is not without problems either. Even as the United States adopted a more confrontational stance under the Reagan administration, it continued to engage in cooperative interactions with the Soviet Union, including on major arms control initiatives like the INF treaty. Furthermore, and in direct contradiction to Rummel's claims, recent scholarship demonstrates that increased interaction does have a positive impact on peace. Research has consistently shown that countries with higher levels of membership in international organizations and greater levels of economic interdependence, for example, are less likely to experience militarized disputes (Oneal & Russett, 1997). Rummel's findings likely diverge from those of other scholars because his analysis does not control for contiguity and geographic distance. Countries are more likely to go to war with their neighbors. Once that factor is taken into account, we find that increased economic interaction is associated with reduction in militarized conflict. Since Rummel's time it has become standard practice in modern analyses of liberal peace theory to control for contiguity and distance.

On the other hand, Rummel was right about much. The shift from détente to rollback under the Reagan administration—a new strategy that reflected many of Rummel's suggestions—did presage the end of the Cold War. During the 1980s, the United States engaged in a campaign of foreign interventions aimed not just at countering Soviet aggression, as in Afghanistan in 1979, but actively 'rolling back' communist and leftist governments. These interventions, including the invasion of Granada (1983), the bombing of Libya (1986), and the provision of arms and funds to the Contras in Nicaragua (1982), were designed to signal American intent and credibility. Meanwhile, Washington rebuilt its military forces, such that by 1986, it had surpassed the Soviet Union in terms of military expenditure (Noren, 2007). This campaign of defense spending, including reinstatement of the B-1 Lancer program, production of LGM-118 Peacekeeper missile, and investment in the Strategic Defense Initiative, eventually convinced the Soviet Union that it could no longer spend itself into exhaustion.

Did the United States win the Cold War because it followed a path similar to the one Rummel advocated or despite doing so? This chapter, of course, will not be able to resolve longstanding debates about the drivers of the Soviet Union's collapse, but it can evaluate the impact of the ideas contained in *Peace Endangered* for other issues in contemporary scholarship and policy. The rest of the article will, therefore, consider the implications of Rummel's views of power, arms control, and nuclear deterrence.

Rummel's definition of power as the product of a nation's capability, intent, and credibility is a nuanced take on an often-oversimplified concept. It is a formulation that casts light on seemingly inexplicable outcomes. Why, despite overwhelming advantages in terms of military technology, training, and manpower, did the United States falter in Vietnam (and the Soviet Union in Afghanistan)? Why was Adolf Hitler not deterred by British and French threats despite the overwhelming power of the alliance that they were able to bring together just a few years later? Why was Iran able to continue to enrich uranium despite demands from all five United Nations Security Council members that it suspend its program?

Rummel's formulation of power suggests an answer: many 'asymmetrical' conflicts are not asymmetrical at all. When intent, resolve, and credibility are taken into account, the seemingly weaker actor may even have the advantage.

This is a theme that has been picked up and extended by contemporary scholars. Arreguin-Toft (2005) has explained how the weak win wars. Press (2005) has argued that both power and interests must be taken into account in order to understand the credibility of military threats. And models of inter-state crises continue to focus on the interaction of resolve and capabilities (Fearon, 1995). For example, a recent comprehensive empirical examination by one of the authors of this article shows that, much as Rummel might have hypothesized, both the balance of resolve and the balance of nuclear forces are critical determinants of nuclear crisis outcomes (Kroenig, 2013).

It is precisely because of the multidimensional nature of power that arms control agreements so often break down, which Rummel believed would be inevitable. As his statistical analysis demonstrated, merely restraining a nation's military capability will not necessarily change its attitudes or manufacture goodwill from thin air; in fact, the causal effect often runs the opposite way. As Ronald Reagan was fond of saying about the US-Soviet relationship, 'We do not distrust each other because we are armed, we are armed because we distrust each other' (Reagan, 1985). In other words, arms races are often the product of conflicts of interest rather than the cause of them. By failing to recognize this dynamic, arms control regimes often do not address the root of the problem.

By the logic of Détente 2, for example, the ratification of the New START treaty in 2010 should have ushered in a period of reduced tensions between Washington and Moscow. Yet instead of a 'reset', we have seen in recent years a rapid deterioration in the relationship. The countries have engaged in policy clashes including Russia's invasion of Ukraine and threats to the rest of NATO. Russia has flouted its obligations under existing arms control regimes, testing a new intermediate-range, ground-launched cruise missile (GLCM) in direct violation of the 1987 INF treaty. Moreover, Russia's long-range RS-26 ballistic missile program can also be operated at intermediate range, allowing the country a technical circumvention of the agreement. These developments are part and parcel of a new and more assertive Russian foreign policy.

Some hoped that the rise of the Islamic State in Iraq and Syria (ISIS) would bring Washington and Moscow together through a common interest in battling Islamic extremism, but the interests here too are misaligned. While both would prefer to defeat ISIS, they have fundamentally different preferences for how best to go about it. Russia's foremost goal is to prop up embattled Syrian dictator Bashar al Assad, while Washington believes that ISIS can only be defeated after Assad is ousted from power.

It is this clash of interests between Washington and Moscow that renders Russian policymakers resistant to arms control measures. Arms control is predicated in part upon the notion that bad relations arise from the uncertain haze of the security dilemma. By allowing nations to signal their benign intent in a controlled manner, arms control regimes seek to clear this haze. Yet, because the ongoing tension between Washington and Moscow stems from a misalignment of interests rather than a misunderstanding of them, arms control regimes like New START and INF merely address the symptoms, not the causes, of conflict.

Indeed, the risk of nuclear war between the United States and Russia might be higher now than at any time since the Cold War. To understand why, let us revisit Rummel's discussion of the necessary conditions for bilateral deterrence. According to Rummel, deterrence requires strength in conventional, tactical and strategic capabilities. A gap at any of these levels creates an opening for an

opponent to exploit, encouraging aggression and making war more likely. It also makes conflict more likely to escalate when it does occur. If a defending nation has a missing rung in the escalation ladder, it may be forced to reach for a higher rung. In this way, a conventional war can evolve into a tactical nuclear one, and a limited nuclear exchange can spiral into strategic exchange.

This account of nuclear deterrence has direct implications for the US-Russian relationship today, for several reasons. First, Russia has undertaken a massive modernization of and reinvestment in its nuclear forces, including new long-range, nuclear-armed cruise missiles, submarine-launched ballistic missiles (SLBMs), and silo-based and road-mobile ICBMs. Second, Russia has moved nuclear weapons to the center of its national security strategy and military doctrine. In 2000, Russia revised its nuclear 'no first use' doctrine to allow for 'de-escalatory' nuclear strikes. While this language was excluded from Russia's most recent public documents, the mentality of 'escalate to de-escalate' persists in Russian military circles and Russian officials have not shied away from issuing explicit nuclear threats (Kroenig, 2015a, b).

Moreover, even as Russia strengthens its nuclear capability and doctrine, the United States and NATO have moved in the opposite direction, deemphasizing nuclear weapons as a tool of statecraft. As it stands, NATO maintains a strong conventional force, a robust strategic nuclear capability and a significant gap in the middle, leaving Russia with a significant battlefield nuclear advantage. The tactical nuclear gap between Washington and Moscow, as Rummel would argue, encourages Russia's model of hybrid warfare, a combination of low-level aggression backstopped by threats of early nuclear escalation.

Moreover, US and NATO tactical deficiency puts it in a difficult situation should war break out. If the United States becomes embroiled in conflict in Ukraine or a NATO member country, and Russia opts for a limited nuclear strike, a US president would have few good options for a tailored, sub-strategic response. Under the current strategy in Europe, much as in Rummel's time, we in the West are 'seriously deteriorating our nuclear retaliatory capability while increasingly relying on an incredible massive retaliation threat' (Rummel, 1976: viii). A Russian tactical strike might very well then force a choice between 'war or surrender' (Rummel, 1976: ix).

The solution, Rummel would argue, would be for NATO to develop a more credible nuclear response option. Possibilities proposed by one of the authors of this article include placing lower-yield nuclear warheads on existing SLBMs and ICBMs, bringing back a sea-launched nuclear cruise missile, or rotationally basing B-52 bombers and nuclear air-launched cruise missiles in Europe (Kroenig, 2015a, b). By signaling US and NATO capability and credibility to Moscow, a strengthened nuclear capability could deter Russian aggression and help avert nuclear exchange.

Of course, for many, nuclear war remains an unthinkable prospect. But, as Rummel writes, 'From our contemporary viewpoint some aspects of the future always will be unthinkable.' The job of scholars and practitioners of national security is in part to anticipate and prepare for the kinds of scenarios that 'would not be accepted as a realistic novel' (Rummel, 1976: 17). The strength of Rummel's work lies in his willingness to engage with such ideas.

Although Rummel's bold analysis caused him to ring some false alarms, it just as often led to conclusions that have stood the test of time. As the West faces a resurgent Russia and a new generation of scholars flocks to issues of nuclear deterrence and arms control, Rummel's *A Peace Endangered* continues to deserve a prominent place on our bookshelves.

References

Arreguin-Toft, Ivan (2005) *How the Weak Win Wars: A Theory of Asymmetric Conflict*. Cambridge: Cambridge University Press.

Fearon, James D (1995) Rationalist explanations of war. *International Organization* 49(3): 379–414.

Kroenig, Matthew (2013) Nuclear superiority and the balance of resolve: Explaining nuclear crisis outcomes. *International Organization* 67(1): 141–171.

Kroenig, Matthew (2015a) Facing reality: Getting NATO ready for a new cold war. *Survival* 57 (1): 49–70.

Kroenig, Matthew (2015b) Statement of Dr. Matthew Kroenig before Senate Armed Services Committee Hearing on 'Regional Nuclear Dynamics', http://www.armed-services.senate.gov/hearings/15-02-25-regional-nuclear-dynamics.

Natural Resources Defense Council (2006) Global nuclear stockpiles,1945–2006, *Bulletin of the Atomic Scientists* 62(4): 64–66.

Noren, James (2007) CIA's Analysis of the Soviet economy. In: Gerald K Haines & Robert E Leggett (eds) *Watching the Bear: Essays on CIA's Analysis of the Soviet Union*. Washington, DC: Center for the Study of Intelligence, http://www.cia.gov/library/center-for-the-study-of-intelligence/csi-publications/books-and-monographs/watching-the-bear-essays-on-cias-analysis-of-the-soviet-union/article02.html.

Oneal, John R & Bruce M Russett (1997) The classical liberals were right: Democracy, interdependence, and conflict, 1950–1985. *International Studies Quarterly* 41(2): 267–294

Press, Daryl G (2005) *Calculating Credibility: How Leaders Assess Military Threats*. Ithaca, NY: Cornell University Press.

Reagan, Ronald (1985) *Address to the Nation on the Upcoming Soviet-United States Summit Meeting in Geneva*, http://www.reagan.utexas.edu/archives/speeches/1985/111485d.htm.

Rummel, Rudolph J (1976) *Peace Endangered: The Reality of Détente*. London: Sage.

Chapter 7
Rummel's Unfinished Legacy: Reconciling Peace Research and Realpolitik

Erich Weede

7.1 The Legacy

Rudy Rummel consistently was a bold and innovative scholar. In the 1960s, the field of international relations was still in the grip of contemporary and diplomatic historians or international lawyers. This did not satisfy him. He looked for a more scientific approach modeled on the natural sciences. He wrote one of the first dissertations that may be labeled as quantitative international politics or scientific peace research. His 'Dimensionality of Nations Project' (Rummel, 1972) was one of the early big data collection efforts in international politics. As far as I can see, he was one of the first (or even the first) to make the dyad instead of the nation state into his most important unit of analysis (Rummel, 1977). Today it is hard to imagine quantitative research in international politics without analyzing dyads. Psychometrics rather than econometrics provided the research paradigm in the early days of the quantitative approach to world politics. That is why much of Rummel's work relied on factor analysis which is a basic tool of psychometrics. By contrast, current quantitative research on international relations is more influenced by econometrics where regression is the most basic tool. His methodological innovations first attracted me to Rummel and his work. He also permitted me to use his data base for my quantitative dissertation project. Having had some education in psychometrics before I turned to political science and international relations, his approach to the field looked plausible and convincing, even paradigmatic to me.

Important as his methodological innovations have been, he also contributed to substantive theory. The intellectual roots of the democratic peace theory date back

Erich Weede, b. 1942 in Hildesheim (Germany), taught sociology at the Universities of Cologne and Bonn (1978–2004) after acquiring academic degrees in psychology and political science. In 1982–83 he was president of the Peace Science Society (International), and in 1985–86 vice-president of the International Studies Association. His books include *Economic Development, Social Order and World Politics* (Lynne Rienner, 1996) and *The Balance of Power, Globalization, and the Capitalist Peace* (Friedrich-Naumann-Stiftung, 2004); Email: e.weede@uni-bonn.de.

© The Author(s) 2017   61
N.P. Gleditsch (ed.), *R.J. Rummel: An Assessment of His Many Contributions*,
SpringerBriefs on Pioneers in Science and Practice 37,
DOI 10.1007/978-3-319-54463-2_7

at least to the 18th century, and another American scholar revived interest in the idea shortly before Rudy, but it was *his* work that instigated an explosion of interest and research on the topic. Although nothing is beyond dispute in the social sciences, Rummel's view on the existence of a democratic peace has become the dominant view among contemporary researchers. Later, Rummel expanded his research agenda. He no longer investigated only wars or deadly quarrels, but mass murder or 'death by government' (Rummel, 1994). In his view: 'Freedom inhibits violence' (Rummel, 1979: 292). Whereas many or most adherents of the democratic peace theory may be labeled 'doves' or even 'leftists', these labels never fitted Rudy. He was a staunch anti-Communist during the Cold War (Rummel, 1976) and a hawk even beyond it. He was a libertarian and a believer in limited government. Although his work did never really focus on 'the capitalist peace', one may regard this more recent line of thinking and research as a continuation of his work. Certainly, it fits his libertarian spirit.

This sketch of Rummel's research agenda and conclusions raises the question: How can one simultaneously be a libertarian and a hawk? Libertarians want to minimize government. Hawkish foreign policies cannot avoid expanding government, at least military establishments. To put the same issue into a slightly different perspective: Most hawks are adherents of the realist approach to world politics. Like Rummel, realists believe in military power, not in soft power. Are Rummel's views consistent? They might be, if one assumes that enemies exist, that they are not merely products of misguided imagination. Here, Rummel (1979: 292) himself provides some cues in his writing: 'Libertarian systems are the natural enemies of authoritarian and totalitarian states. By their example and the products of freedom they are naturally subversive of authoritarian and totalitarian systems; and these freedoms seem to make libertarian states defenseless against unilateral changes in the status quo.' Like realists, he worried about challenges to national security, deterrence, and defense. Since I largely share his views and also combine libertarianism with a certain degree of hawkishness, I shall dare to attempt to reconcile what many or even most political scientists regard as irreconcilable. Russian aggression or the persistent crisis in the Ukraine provides the background for my attempt. Being a hawk, Rummel was close to realism. Nevertheless, he was not a member of that school of thought. Otherwise, he would have been more interested in the distinction between vital and peripheral interests, in power transitions and the decline of nations, and in spheres of influence.

7.2   Russian Expansion in the Ukraine: A Realist View

Using the label 'realist' does not necessarily say that 'realist' theorizing is true, or at least better than other theories. But there is probably no view of world politics that is more widely accepted than realism among national security elites of the great powers. The starting point of realism is the belief in the existence of a 'security dilemma' or an 'anarchical order of power'. Since there is no effective authority which can impose order and peace on great powers, states have to take security into their own hands. They have to prepare for the worst, i.e., aggression by other powers.

The obvious strategy is to seek 'security by superiority' or 'peace by strength'. Unfortunately, it is inconceivable that all great powers are superior to all others and therefore safe. Superiority is a positional good. Claiming it for oneself implies denial to others. Therefore, realists regard world politics as a 'tragedy'. In contrast to many adherents and promoters of the democratic peace, they consider moralizing dangerous, more likely to enhance risks of war than to diminish them. Realism is descriptive as well as prescriptive. According to Mearsheimer (2001: 12), 'Although there is much truth in the description of great powers as prisoners trapped in an iron cage, the fact remains that they sometimes—although not often—act in contradiction to the theory. ... As we shall see, such foolish behavior invariably has negative consequences.' From a realist point of view it is important not to let moral judgments cloud the distinction between vital interests which might merit a fight and lesser interests which could detract one's attention from more important issues.

The Russian take-over of the Crimea, Russian support of separatism in the Eastern Ukraine, and Russian destabilization of the Ukraine alarmed Western politicians. Before 2014 Russia was believed to be—or, at least, hoped to be—a status quo power and resigned to its loss of influence in its near-abroad. Politicians in the West rarely thought about red lines which might exist in Putin's or other influential Russian minds. NATO and the EU expanded, in the Baltic even including three states which had been forced to be part of the Soviet Union itself. In contrast to the small Baltic republics, however, the Ukraine was not a victor's booty after World War II. The historical link between the Ukraine and Russia is deep. Talk about Ukrainian NATO membership, and later about a special relationship with the EU must have raised alarm bells in Moscow. But many European politicians are so innocent of familiarity with realist thinking that they could not imagine that Russia did simply not believe in the pacific self-image of the EU. Realists in Moscow observed relentless NATO and EU expansion into former Soviet territory and assumed the worst about Western intentions. In order to forestall an imagined Western expansion, Russia itself expanded.

Should the West do something about it, or should it take consolation from the proposition that Russia is a declining power for demographic, geopolitical[1] and economic reasons that does not need to be contained? If Russia were a declining power, and if Western reactions to Russian expansion or aggression could make Russia align with a rising power likely to challenge the West in future, i.e., China, then containing Russia would be a mistake, then this would be 'foolish', or a failure to distinguish between vital and peripheral interests (Mearsheimer, 2014a). The only

---

[1]According to some geopolitical theories (Bernholz, 1985; Collins, 1986: 167–185), accessibility to other great powers or an interior location in the configuration of great powers is a disadvantage, whereas a peripheral or marshland location is an advantage. Russia currently has the least favorable geopolitical location of all great powers or candidates for great power status. It faces China and Japan in the East, and Europe in the West. By contrast, the US has the most favorable location. It is surrounded by oceans rather than being close to other great powers. Collins (1986: 167ff) predicted the future decline of the Russian empire. Since he underlines the continuity between Muscovy, Tsarist Russia, and the Soviet Union, it is plausible to extend his geopolitical arguments to Putin's Russia.

significant consequence of containing China might be assisting the rise of China. From a 'realist' point of view, the West should not treat Russia as a permanent adversary and thereby turn it into one. As Mearsheimer (2014b: 89) has observed: 'The United States will also someday need Russia's help containing a rising China.'

7.3 Realism and the Capitalist Peace

Although 'realism' is the dominant school of thought in international relations, it is not the only one. According to realism, the security dilemma condemns mankind to live with the risk of war forever. Since realists focus on conflicts of interest, they might nevertheless (or: therefore?) empathize better with opponents than others.[2] In debating NATO expansion eastwards, some realists are less expansionist than others (Mearsheimer, 2014b). In the nuclear age, admitting that great power politics remains a tragedy is not attractive. A rival school of thought is sometimes called 'idealism' or 'liberalism'. It is more optimistic. In contrast to realism, it even provides some hope for avoiding a clash of Chinese and Western civilizations. According to this line of thinking, either economic interdependence or democratization or both may significantly reduce the risk of war. From this perspective, globalization is useful by spreading interdependence and prosperity first and, possibly, democratization later. For some time quantitative research (Gartzke, 2005, 2007; Russett & Oneal, 2001; summarized by Weede, 2011) has demonstrated that the risk of war between nations is reduced, if they trade a lot with each other. There is something like a commercial peace or peace by trade.[3] Until recently the debate among researchers was whether the commercial or capitalist peace is as strong as the democratic peace. Now, the ground is shifting toward the question which aspects of a capitalist order promote the avoidance of war most effectively: Is it trade or the expectation of future free trade (Copeland, 2015)? Or, is it the avoidance of protectionism? Or, is it the avoidance of state ownership of the means of production, of state-owned enterprises (McDonald, 2007)? Or, is it financial market openness and economic freedom (Gartzke, 2005, 2007)? All of these specific interpretations of the general idea of a capitalist or commercial peace seem to justify some optimism about the effects of globalization or the export of capitalism from the West to the rest of the world. In particular, it should be underlined that economic cooperation pacifies the relationship between a rising China and the West.

---

[2]See, for example, Gelb (2015: 10): 'It is totally unrealistic, however, to think that the West can gain desired Russian restraint and cooperation without dealing with Moscow as a great power that possesses real and legitimate interests, especially in its border areas.' Obviously, the Ukraine is the most important border area for Russia.

[3]Copeland (2015: Chap. 2) reads the quantitative literature somewhat differently from me. But he agrees with me on the fact that most researchers see economic interdependence as a pacifying condition and that the democratic peace is anchored in economic cooperation. He focuses on interactions which permit interdependence to increase or decrease conflict contingent on conditioning variables.

One could even conceptualize the democratic peace as a component of the capitalist peace (Weede, 2011), because democracies prosper best in wealthy countries, because capitalism or economic freedom and thereby globalization contribute to prosperity. Since rising powers tend to challenge the political status quo (Organski, 1958; Organski & Kugler, 1980), it is good luck that the still dominant US and rising China seem to prosper under global capitalism, that they trade a lot with each other and are economically interdependent.

Since neither realist nor liberal—or, in Rummel's terms, libertarian—hopes for peace based on economic interdependence, prosperity, and democracy present a full picture of world politics, one has to face the question whether realist and liberal convictions can be reconciled. A prerequisite for reconciling these seemingly irreconcilable views might be the recognition of spheres of influence (Etzioni, 2015).[4] During the Cold War the Western alliance system was something like an American sphere of influence, and according to Brzezinski (1997: 53) this remained true beyond it, whereas the Warsaw Pact was the Soviet sphere of influence. Deterrence could work because both sides understood where the red lines were. Recognition of spheres of influence comes easily to realists, but is more difficult for liberals or peace researchers who are interested in human rights and democracy. But the capitalist peace, including the democratic peace, may be attainable only, if the West recognizes that non-democratic great powers, including Russia, insist on maintaining spheres of influence. Except for North Korea and the South China Sea the outlines of China's sphere of influence are not yet clarified. In Moscow or Beijing, a Western denial of Russian or Chinese spheres of influence looks indistinguishable from a Western claim to global hegemony.

7.4 Beyond Rummel: Dovish Realism

Russia always considered the Ukraine to be part of its sphere. Western attempts to offer the Ukraine, but not Russia itself, the long-run prospect of EU or even NATO membership could only alienate Russia. Western economic sanctions against Russia cannot promote the economic interdependence and common prosperity on which a capitalist peace between Europe or the West and Russia might be built. Nor would Western sanctions promote democracy in Russia. Only Western recognition of the Ukraine being a part of Moscow's sphere of influence might give interdependence between Europe or the West on the one hand and Russia and the Ukraine on the other hand a chance to reduce tensions and to promote peace. As suggested by a Russian writer associated with the Ministry of Foreign Affairs (Lukin, 2014: 93), 'Finlandization' of the Ukraine might be one way to reconcile Western and Russian

---

[4]Copeland (2015) provides an alternative approach. In his argument, the pacifying impact derives from expectations about the future rather than from the present state of affairs. I cannot imagine that Western sanctions today make Russians, or even the Chinese, more likely to expect lasting benefits from interdependence with the West.

interests. Whereas Finns were personally as free as Western citizens, the West accepted during the Cold War that Finnish NATO membership would be incompatible with Russian national interest. If the West succeeded in making the Ukraine part of the EU and the West, this would be perceived by Russians as a new 'iron curtain' dividing the traditional Russian empire. Alienating Russia by expanding the West into the Ukraine without co-opting Russia at the same time would be a Western gift to China because China could welcome Russia in its sphere of influence.[5]

In essence, advocates of sanctions against Russia neglect many types of cost. First, they forget that Russia might become a partner of a rising China. Second, they forget that sanctions necessarily reduce economic interdependence between Russia and the West and thereby weaken a pacifying factor, possibly the only pacifying factor, in Russian-Western relations. Western sanctions against Russia are even likely to undermine the Chinese hope for future resource or market access within the Western sphere of influence and thereby reduce even the prospects of Western-Chinese peace. Third, advocates of sanctions forget the boomerang effect (Coyne & Hall, 2014) or the impact of sanctions on the character of Western economies. Inevitably, sanctions require Western governments to expand regulation and to interfere even more with the economy. It is dubious whether bigger government is the solution to Western economic problems. Should the West incur these costs, if there is very little hope that sanctions work and achieve their objectives?[6]

As Huntington (1996) has underlined, the United States and Europe (including Poland and the Baltic states) belong to the same civilization. From this perspective, the Atlantic Alliance looks natural, certainly more natural than Putin's vision of a Greater Europe running from Lisbon to Vladivostok where Russia could hope to play a leading role.[7] From an American perspective and, possibly, from a British perspective, too, a united Greater Europe from Lisbon to Vladivostok would transform the fruits of victory in two world wars and the succeeding cold war into a nightmare. Gray (1986: 17) has characterized the foreign policy goals of the Anglophone sea-powers in these terms: 'The same rationale that for four hundred years moved

---

[5]Here, I strongly disagree with Brzezinski (1997: 56) who argues: 'If a choice must be made between a larger Europe-Atlantic system and a better relationship with Russia, the former must rank higher.' But I do endorse the view of Mearsheimer (2014b: 87): 'The United States and its allies should abandon their plan to westernize Ukraine and instead aim to make it a neutral buffer between NATO and Russia, akin to Austria's position during the Cold War.'

[6]According to the empirical literature (Hufbauer, Schott, Elliott & Oegg, 1997; Morgan, Bapat & Krustev, 2009; Pape, 1997; Whang & Kim, 2015) contentions about their effectiveness vary, but include some devastating comments, such as: 'In most cases a state imposing sanctions on its opponent can expect an outcome that is just about the same as would be obtained without sanctions.' (Morgan & Schwebach, 1997: 46) Moreover, even Hufbauer et al. who do assert that economic sanctions sometimes work, admit that they tend to be least effective against strong, stable, autocratic, and hostile targets. As Simes (2014: 11) pointed out, even resolute sanctions against Cuba, North Korea, Iraq, or Iran did not produce the desired result. One should expect Russia to be somewhat less vulnerable to sanctions than these much smaller countries. The American oil embargo against Japan before World War II may even have contributed to the subsequent war.

[7]Lukin (2015: 65) recently called for 'a pan-European center of power based on three legs: Paris, Berlin and Moscow'.

British statesmen to join or organize coalitions to deny continental hegemony, has been the publicly under-acknowledged geopolitical Leitmotiv for American international security policy since 1917 (though with an extensive lapse in the interwar period). A continental super-state would be able, if unopposed by land, to translate superior land power into what might become superior sea power … From a geopolitical perspective, the Soviet challenge to American security is the same as was the German.' If one puts aside the demographic weakness of most of Europe as well as of Russia, then Putin's plans for Greater Europe—though unlikely ever to be realized— would be a worse challenge to Atlantic sea-power than previous historical challenges. One should also consider, however, that the inclusion of Russia in a Chinese sphere of influence might be even worse from an American perspective than Putin's dreams about Eurasia. Given the decline of Europe and Japan, and the economic head-start of China over India, future struggles for hegemony will put China against the United States. A core issue of the future hegemonic rivalry concerns whether the Russian natural resource treasure chest will become more easily accessible to Europe and the West or to China. By not conceding a sphere of influence to Russia now, in Ukraine and elsewhere in Russia's near-abroad, the West might push Russia into a nascent Chinese sphere. Simultaneously, Western economic sanctions against Russia might teach ascending China the lesson that economic interdependence with the West might be incompatible with its national interest.

7.5 Rummel's Strategic Environment and Ours

Rudy's research program and his strategic views evolved during the cold war. Bipolarity and the mutual balance of terror looked like persistent characteristics of the strategic environment. Under these conditions, the tension between libertarianism or the promotion of the democratic peace and deterrence or balancing the Soviet Union was limited. Libertarianism and the democratic peace were applicable within the West. Realism and the need for 'security by superiority' were essential towards the Soviet Union. Currently, the strategic situation is different. Bipolarity has gone, the Soviet Union has disappeared. But China is rising. Of course, no one can know, whether Rudy would have made an argument like this or developed an entirely different one. But we do know that he would have had a definite view on the Ukrainian crisis and been outspoken about it. Ultimately, his legacy is his example. He was not afraid of a new research paradigm, nor of offending the strategic consensus of the multitude who never even thought of doing research.

References

Bernholz, Peter (1985) *The International Game of Power*. Berlin: Mouton.
Brzezinski, Zbigniew (1997) A geostrategy for Eurasia. *Foreign Affairs* 76(5): 50–64.
Collins, Randall (1986) *Weberian Sociological Theory*. New York: Cambridge University Press.
Copeland, Dale C (2015) *Economic Interdependence and War*. Princeton, NJ: Princeton University Press.

Coyne, Christopher J & Abigail R Hall (2014) Perfecting tyranny: Foreign intervention as experimentation in state control. *Independent Review* 19(2): 165–189.

Etzioni, Amitai (2015) Spheres of influence: A reconceptualization. *Fletcher Forum of World Affairs* 39 (2): 117–132.

Gartzke, Erik (2005) Freedom and peace. In: James D Gwartney & Robert A Lawson (eds) *Economic Freedom in the World*. Vancouver, BC: Fraser Institute, 29–44.

Gartzke, Erik (2007) The capitalist peace. *American Journal of Political Science* 51(1): 166–191.

Gelb, Leslie H (2015) Détente plus. *National Interest* 138: 9–21.

Gray, Colin S (1986) *Maritime Strategy, Geopolitics, and the Defense of the West*. New York: Ramapo Press, for National Strategy Information Center.

Hufbauer, Gary Clyde; Jeffrey J Schott, Kimberly Ann Elliott & Barbara Oegg (1997) *Economic Sanctions Reconsidered*. 3rd ed. Washington, DC: Peterson Institute for International Economics.

Huntington, Samuel P (1996) *The Clash of Civilizations and the Remaking of World Order*. New York: Simon and Schuster.

Lukin, Alexander (2014) What the Kremlin is thinking. Putin's vision for Eurasia. *Foreign Affairs* 93 (4): 85–93.

Lukin, Vladimir (2015) Looking west from Russia. *National Interest* 140: 59–65.

McDonald, Patrick J (2007) The purse strings of peace. *American Journal of Political Science* 51(3): 569–582.

Mearsheimer, John J (2001) *The Tragedy of Great Power Politics*. New York: Norton.

Mearsheimer, John J (2014a) America unhinged. *National Interest* 129: 9–30.

Mearsheimer, John J (2014b) Why the Ukraine crisis is the West's fault. The liberal illusions that provoked Putin. *Foreign Affairs* 93(5): 77–89.

Morgan, T Clifton & Valerie L Schwebach (1997) Fools suffer gladly: The use of economic sanctions in international crises. *International Studies Quarterly* 41(1): 27–50.

Morgan, T Clifton; Navin Bapat & Valentin Krustev (2009) The threat and imposition of economic sanctions, 1971–2000. *Conflict Management and Peace Science* 26(1): 92–110.

Organski, AFK (1958) *World Politics*. New York: Knopf.

Organski, AFK & Jacek Kugler (1980) *The War Ledger*. Chicago, IL: University of Chicago Press.

Pape, Robert A (1997) Why sanctions do not work. *International Security* 22(2): 90–136.

Rummel, RJ (1972) *The Dimensions of Nations*. Beverly Hills, CA: Sage.

Rummel, RJ (1976) *Peace Endangered. The Reality of Détente*. Beverly Hills, CA: Sage.

Rummel, RJ (1977) *Field Theory Evolving*. Beverly Hills, CA: Sage.

Rummel, RJ (1979) Understanding Conflict and War. Vol. 4: *War, Power, Peace*. Beverly Hills, CA: Sage.

Rummel, RJ (1994) *Death by Government*. New Brunswick, NJ: Transaction.

Russett, Bruce M & John R Oneal (2001) *Triangulating Peace: Democracy, Interdependence and International Organizations*. New York: Norton.

Simes, Dimitri K (2014) Reawakening an empire. *National Interest* (132): 5–15.

Weede, Erich (2011) The capitalist peace. In: Christopher J Coyne & Rachel L Mathers (eds) *Handbook on the Political Economy of War*. Northampton, MA: Edward Elgar, 269–280.

Whang, Taehee & Hannah June Kim (2015) International signaling and economic sanctions. *International Interactions* 41(3): 427–452.

Chapter 8
Understanding Conflict and War: An Overlooked Classic?

James Lee Ray

8.1 Introduction

Soon after it was published, a perspicacious review of R.J. Rummel's *Understanding Conflict and War* (UCW)[1] predicted that the work would 'not have the immediate impact … that one might otherwise expect from a work of such scope written by one of the more famous names in the field' (Ray, 1982: 185). By 1988, Rummel himself acknowledged regarding UCW that 'I did not expect it to be a hit', but that 'I was not prepared … for UCW to be so widely ignored' (personal correspondence).

Nevertheless, Rummel received 15 research grants, authored over 70 articles, and 21 books, one of which (*Applied Factor Analysis*, 1970), was selected by the Institute of Scientific Information as a 'Citation Classic', so the point here is not that Rummel in general labored in vain or in obscurity. But subsequent to the publication of UCW, the democratic peace proposition received an enormous amount of attention. Unfortunately, even when Rummel's contribution to the formulation and exposition of this idea is recognized, the specific citations are usually limited to a couple of derivative articles, published after UCW (i.e., Rummel 1983, 1985). And Rummel's role in bringing the democratic peace proposition to the fore is far from universally recognized. For example, Spiro (1994: 50) asserts that 'the absence of wars among liberal democracies was noted before (Doyle, 1983), but it was not

James Lee Ray, b. 1944, Ph.D. in Political Science (University of Michigan, 1974); Emeritus Professor, Department of Political Science, Vanderbilt University (2013–); author of *Democracy and International Conflict* (University of South Carolina Press, 1995, 1998), and articles in *British Journal of Political Science, International Organization, International Studies Quarterly, Journal of Democracy, and Journal of Peace Research*; current main interests: golf, fishing, movies, and power naps; Email: james.l.ray@vanderbilt.edu.

[1]This chapter is a shortened and revised version of Ray (1998). Material from this article is reprinted by permission of the publisher. Several contributors to this volume made comments for the 2015 ISA panel devoted to R.J. Rummel's work that are reflected in the revisions. Nils Petter Gleditsch offered several specific and useful revisions and suggestions.

© The Author(s) 2017   69
N.P. Gleditsch (ed.), *R.J. Rummel: An Assessment of His Many Contributions*,
SpringerBriefs on Pioneers in Science and Practice 37,
DOI 10.1007/978-3-319-54463-2_8

seen as confirmation of any particular theory', an intriguing statement in light of the five volumes of theoretical (as well as metaphysical and epistemological) elaboration upon which the democratic peace proposition is based in UCW.

The point of this chapter is that, especially in light of the subsequent level of interest in the democratic peace proposition, perhaps there are additional aspects of UCW that merit a more thorough consideration than they have received to date. I will highlight some of the theoretical notions and empirical implications to be found in UCW that are arguably especially undeserving of the absence of attention they have received. A special emphasis will be placed on the aspects of UCW that resonate with more current work, in complementary or competing ways.

8.2   UCW: Structure and Main Themes

The first of Rummel's five volumes, *The Dynamic Psychological Field*, addresses basic questions regarding human behavior. Rummel argues that it is a function of dispositions weighted by expectations, and also of personality weighted by perceived situations. He then places individuals within a sociocultural context, stressing that personality, society, and culture form a continuous whole, and that they interact within a 'field'. It is here, too, that Rummel begins to develop a theme about the importance of status as a determinant of an individual's behavior.

This first volume also dwells at some length on the question of whether or not people have a 'free will'. He feels that most social scientists tend to see the behavior of human beings as determined. He resolves this dilemma for social science, at least to his own satisfaction, by arguing that the human will is free at the underlying level of 'things-in-themselves', while at the level of phenomena it is determined, thus making it a suitable target for scientific investigation. The first volume concludes with the development of a metaphysical, epistemological framework called 'intentional humanism', which integrates human perceptions, attitudes, personality traits, and needs with sociocultural, physical, and biophysical surroundings.

In the second volume, *The Conflict Helix*, Rummel focuses on human interaction, and on the impact of distance with respect to status on relationships between social entities. He also differentiates between types of power. Bargaining power is distinguished from coercive power, and from authoritative power. What distinguishes national societies from each other most fundamentally, according to Rummel, is the type of power that is most prevalent in relationships within those societies. Bargaining power is the basis for exchange societies; authoritative power predominates in closed, aristocratic, or traditional societies; while coercive power is the most important distinguishing characteristic of totalitarian political systems, in which elites use such power to propel society toward some ideologically inspired goal. Rummel's analysis of empirical data leads him to conclude that these ideal types do in fact conform to the existence of exchange (or libertarian, or democratic), authoritative, and totalitarian political systems in the 'real world'.

In the third volume, *Conflict in Perspective*, Rummel compares his theory of conflict and violence with others, and concludes that his is superior to or subsumes the most prominent alternatives. He argues that his theory suggests that aggression is both instinctive and learned. Rummel, like Marx, argues that class conflict is important in most societies; however, for Rummel the two most fundamentally important classes are the rulers, on the one hand, and the ruled, on the other. He feels that cross-pressures among groups can mitigate such conflict in exchange societies, but in others class conflict between the rulers and the ruled is also potentially, and often in fact, dramatically violent. Only decentralization, or 'democracy', can solve this problem.

It is in the fourth volume, *War, Power, Peace* that Rummel deals most specifically with international relations in general and international conflict in particular. He offers propositions, as opposed to hypotheses about conflict, which he defines as 'definite affirmations about conflict grounded in a perspective on man's psychology, society, and conflict' (Rummel, 1979: 211), that is, statements that are more definitive and less tentative than hypotheses. There are 54 propositions in all, 33 of which focus specifically on the causes and conditions of conflict. It is in this volume where the democratic peace, or the interdemocratic peace proposition, is first presented.

The Just Peace, the final volume, is devoted to an effort to demonstrate how Rummel's theory of conflict can have a profound impact on the future of international politics. 'My answer ...', he asserts at the outset of the volume, can be put simply: 'promote freedom' (Rummel, 1981: 15). He defends this answer through the development of a social contract model. That model relies importantly on a first principle of John Rawls, which is that a society should be devised and structured in such a way as self-interested people would have it structured if they are ignorant of their own interests and the positions and advantages they would have in that society.

8.3 UCW: System-level Propositions

Neither Rummel's work in general, nor UCW in particular, is generally perceived to be particularly relevant to theoretical nor research concerns focused on the international systemic level of analysis. Nevertheless, there are systemic level implications of the theoretical approach to conflict developed in UCW that are among its unexploited aspects. Among the 33 basic 'theoretical propositions on the causes and conditions of international conflict behavior', there are two that focus on the relationship between polarity and international conflict. The first is 'polarity stimulates intense violence', (Rummel, 1979: 284), and the other is 'polarity inhibits nonviolent conflict and low level violence', (Rummel, 1979: 288). Though these appear contradictory, in fact they jointly posit a curvilinear relationship. Another related proposition relevant to analyses of the international system asserts that 'cross-pressures inhibit intense violence' (Rummel, 1979: 290).

Perhaps the most intriguing derivation from Rummel's theoretical approach in UCW regarding the international system is that 'international relations are an exchange society with a libertarian political system' (Rummel, 1979: 431), and that, accordingly, 'international relations could be better characterized as a state of peace' (Rummel, 1979: 46). Rummel follows up on the implications of such assertions and concludes that in general international politics are on average less violent than domestic politics. He asserts that 'political regimes-governments-have probably murdered nearly 170,000,000 of their own citizens and foreigners in this century-about four times the number killed in all international and domestic wars and revolutions' (Rummel, 1995a: 3).

The implication of Rummel's theory that international politics are on average less violent than domestic politics certainly qualifies as one of those counter-intuitive findings that are supposed to be a hallmark of valid and valuable theory.[2] A related counter-intuitive notion would assert that international law, contrary to continual disparaging remarks to the contrary about it, is actually more effective than domestic law.

In sum, Rummel's UCW has intriguing, mostly unexplored implications for analyses of international politics on the systemic level of analysis.

8.4 Dyadic-level Propositions in UCW and Contemporary Research

Rummel is appropriately identified as a theorist most intently focused on the dyadic level of analysis, and the proposition in UCW that has received the most attention (even if by many who are only dimly aware of UCW), asserts that 'violence does not occur between free societies' (Rummel, 1979: 374).[3]

Quite consistently, Rummel refers to the 'free societies' as 'libertarian' rather than 'democratic'. 'Libertarian' states, by his definition, must rely to a substantial extent on 'free markets.' In other words, socialist states, even if they are 'democratic,' are not 'libertarian,' and therefore may not, in his view be peaceful in their relationships with each other. This theme in UCW is arguably an important precursor to arguments emphasizing the pacifying impact of free markets or capitalism, even as opposed to 'democracy' per se (Gartzke, 2007; Mousseau, 2013). Mousseau in particular, emphasizes the pacifying impact of the degree of 'contract intensity' in a society. Rummel (1976: 310) asserts that an essential feature of 'libertarianism' to which he attributes significant pacifying impact is the 'freedom to contract'.

But there are other dyadic-level propositions in UCW that deserve more attention, partly because they overlap with other important sectors of research on international conflict. This might suggest that the framework developed in UCW has untapped potential to integrate, or even subsume, those other approaches.

For example, an 'age-old theme of international politics' suggests that 'uneven rates of growth in power are the fundamental cause of both war and change in the

---

[2]'A beautiful model is unpredictable. It produces some interesting implications that are surprising to us' (Lave & March, 1975: 61–62).

[3]Rummel goes on to explain that 'violence should almost never occur between exchange societies due to cross-pressures, the diversity of internal groups and interests, and the limited and responsive nature of libertarian government ... In other words, pluralistic democracies with limited government form islands of nonviolent relations' (1979: 374).

international system' (Schweller, 1992: 237). The roots of the idea go back at least to Thucydides. More recently, the idea has been espoused in terms of hegemonic stability theory (Gilpin, 1981), long cycle theory (Modelski, 1978; Goldstein, 1988; Thompson, 1988), theories about preventive war (Levy, 1987), power cycle theory (Doran & Parsons, 1980), and power transition theory (Organski, 1968; Organski & Kugler, 1980). These theories have had a definite tendency to focus on major powers and the impact of transitions as well as re-distributions of power on the international system as a whole; therefore, many of them are perceived as system level theories (see, for example, Midlarsky, 1989). But they focus most intently on dynamics of interaction involving pairs of states. In addition, recent evidence suggests that the logic and impact of power transitions, for example, are not necessarily restricted to major powers, or world hegemons and challengers (Lemke, 1995).

The approach to international conflict developed by Rummel resonates with, could be integrated with, and might even be interpreted as subsuming all of these strands of theoretical work and empirical analyses focusing on the impact of changes in power ratios between states. The first three of the 33 theoretical propositions on the causes and conditions of international conflict behavior presented by Rummel in Volume 4 of UCW are as follows: (1) Conflict Behavior occurs if and only if a mutual structure of expectations is disrupted; (2) Tension and hostility occur if there is a significant shift in the 'balance of powers'; and (3) Conflict Behavior occurs only if there is a significant shift in the 'balance of powers' (Rummel, 1979: 262). These propositions bear an obvious relationship to others focusing on the impact of changes in power distributions or ratios. The relationship is made even stronger by two additional propositions constituting the theoretical edifice developed in UCW, i.e., 'Power parity is correlated with war', and 'An actual or growing weakness of the status quo party compared to the anti-status quo party is particularly correlated with violence' (Rummel, 1979: 264).

Another recent stream of research on international conflict and war has focused on recurring crises and enduring rivalries. Leng (1983, 1993), for example, has analyzed the impact of recurrent crises on the bargaining behavior of the disputants, and vice versa. Gochman & Maoz (1984) note that a large portion of the world's militarized conflict is accounted for by a relatively small number of pairs of states that have come to be known as 'enduring rivals' (Goertz & Diehl, 1992, 1993).

All of this research is obviously congruent with a basic aspect of the theory of conflict developed by Rummel in UCW, namely that 'conflict is helixal'. More specifically, Rummel argues that 'no conflict begins … de novo, without history. Leaders and peoples learn. Each conflict is informed by previous ones … Each successive turn from cooperation to conflict to conflict is at a higher level of experience and insight between the parties; each turn incorporates what was learned before' (Rummel, 1979: 337). There certainly appears here to be substantial room for progress toward theoretical integration of recent work on recurring crises and enduring rivalries and the approach toward international conflict developed by Rummel in UCW.

Another important strand of research on conflict between pairs of states emphasizes the impact of geographic contiguity or proximity as well as territory.

The impact of territorial changes on conflicts between states ties in nicely with research focusing on recurring crises or enduring rivalries. For example, Goertz & Diehl (1992) report that the likelihood of a subsequent conflict between enduring rivals if an episode in the rivalry involves territorial change is affected by various characteristics of that territory and the process by which it is transferred. Similarly Hensel (1994: 281) finds that for enduring rivalries involving Latin American states from 1816 to 1986, 'conflict between the same two adversaries is … more likely when territorial issues are under contention'.

Vasquez (1993) cites several sources pointing out the important impact of contiguity on the probability of war between states (such as Wallensteen, 1981; Diehl, 1985; and Bremer, 1992; another important source of support for the idea is Maoz & Russett, 1993). From this, Vasquez infers the key significance of territory and territorial disputes as factors explaining why some disputes escalate to international war and others do not. Finally, and more recently, Gibler (2012) argues that stable borders are a key to peace. He also argues that stable borders create a spurious relationship between democracy and peace, and thus differentiates his work from Rummel's approach to conflict in striking manner.[4]

Nevertheless, Gibler's work and the entire set of research and theoretical notions regarding the impact of territorial issues and contiguity on international war could be, but virtually never is seen as important validation for the theoretical approach to international conflict developed by Rummel in UCW. One of the basic 33 propositions there on the causes of international conflict is 'geographic distance is negatively correlated with conflict behavior' (Rummel, 1979: 263). Rummel also asserts unequivocally in UCW: 'We thus have three types of status quo: territorial, contractual, and behavioral. *It is only attempts to change the territorial status quo by hostile states that risks violence and war.*' (Rummel, 1979: 177, emphasis in the original)

Recent research on the impact of regime type on conflict between states has taken note of the importance not only of democracy, but of the distance, or differences between states in regime type, to an understanding of the conflict proneness of those states. Oneal & Ray (1997: 751) conclude, for example, that 'the political distance separating states along the democracy-autocracy continuum is an important indicator of the likelihood of dyadic conflict …' Bremer (1996: 28) comes to the similar conclusion that 'political dissimilarity [that is, differences between democracies and autocracies] seems to encourage conflict …'. These findings support Rummel's (1979: 296) argument that 'differences (distance vectors) in wealth, power and politics are of all differences the most correlated with conflict behavior …' and that 'power, wealth and political distance reflect the primary lines of opposition among … states'.

Russett (1995a, b: 268–269) notes that three recent important works on international conflict (Bueno de Mesquita & Lalman, 1992; Maoz, 1990; Vasquez, 1993), have in common the notion that foreign policy decision making 'may vary with international context… But in no case is it purely endogenous to the

---

[4]However, Rummel's emphasis on the importance of a stable status quo to the preservation of peace discussed above is quite congruent with Gibler's work on the impact of stable borders.

international system ...'. Russett goes on to point out that 'the process is likely to be markedly different for different countries. And the process is also importantly interdependent as a dyadic phenomenon.' By this point, the relevance of UCW to this characteristic theme in these three volumes regarding the impact of domestic politics on foreign policy choices, and regarding the importance of analyzing these choices within a dyadic context, should need no more elaboration.

8.5 National-level Hypotheses in UCW

Whether or not democratic states are less war prone, period (a national-level idea) rather than just less war prone in their relationships with each other (a dyadic-level idea) is one of the most important questions to consider in the context of a discussion of Rummel's work on international conflict.[5] Chan (1984) and Weede (1984) challenged Rummel's proposition that libertarianism correlates negatively with degrees of foreign violence, even though neither of them directly evaluated that idea. (Their models focused on war involvement as a dichotomous variable, rather than degrees of violence.) Those articles constitute an important part of the core of findings that lead to the continually repeated assertion that while democratic states do not fight wars against each other, they are as war prone and conflict prone as autocratic states (for two important examples, see Levy, 1988: 661–662 and Gleditsch, 1992: 369–370).

So, the casual, or even the careful reader might understandably conclude that Rummel is a voice in the wilderness calling out against the virtually unanimous opinion and overwhelming evidence that democracies are not less war prone, or conflict prone than nondemocratic states, even though they do not fight wars against each other. But in fact there is substantial evidence to support Rummel's argument that democratic states are less prone to violence, escalation and war than undemocratic states in general, not just in their relationships with each other. A partial list of sources of that evidence would include Geller (1985), Maoz & Russett (1992), Maoz & Abdolali (1989), Morgan & Schwebach (1992), Bueno de Mesquita & Lalman (1992), Bremer (1992), Rousseau, Gelpi, Reiter & Huth (1996), and Benoit (1996) in the more recent era, as well as East & Gregg (1967), Salmore & Hermann (1969), and Zinnes & Wilkenfeld (1971) from earlier decades. Huth (1996: 187), in effect, speaks for all of these sources when he concludes that 'the findings in this book challenge the conventional wisdom that democratic states are only more pacific in their political and military relations with other democracies ...'. If true, this finding tends to disconfirm all those theoretical approaches that imply that democratic states are more peaceful only in their relationships with each other, while it provides support for Rummel's theoretical arguments.

Another reason that Rummel's approach in UCW in general, as well as its national-level ideas in particular, may be deserving of more attention has to do with

---

[5]This section relies extensively on a discussion in Chap. 1 of Ray (1995).

the apparent increasing prevalence of intranational, as opposed to international violence in the contemporary international system. Interpretations of this trend should take into account the fact that intrastate wars have been considerably more common that interstate wars for a long time. Sarkees & Wayman (2010: 564–565) report that there were 95 interstate wars between 1816 and 2007, while during that same time period there were 335 intrastate wars. Furthermore, there were more interstate war onsets than intrastate war onsets in only one decade during this time period (1937–46). Nevertheless 229 out of the 335 intrastate wars occurring between 1816 and 2007 (or 68%) have taken place just since 1982, while only 13 interstate wars began during that same time period. Granted, this proliferation of intrastate wars in recent decades might be accounted for in part by the larger number of states coming into existence in that time period. But the number of *pairs* of states that in principle could have become involved in interstate wars increased much more rapidly in those same decades. If we focus on the most recent data, we see that 'what stands out in the 21st century is the lack of large-scale interstate conflict' (Pettersson & Wallensteen, 2015: 537). In 2014 specifically, there were 40 armed conflicts resulting in at least 25 battle-related deaths, only one of which was an interstate conflict. In that same year, there were 11 wars, with at least 1,000 battle-related deaths, *all* of which were intrastate conflicts. It is particularly interesting, then, that Rummel (1994, 1995a) turned his attention to domestic political strife, and that he did so in a way based on the theoretical approach to conflict developed in UCW.

8.6   Conclusion

One of the basic 33 propositions on the causes and conditions of conflict behavior in UCW asserts that 'intense violence will occur only if there is an expectation of success' (Rummel, 1979: 263). In spite of this potentially important overlap between the approach to conflict developed in UCW and rational choice theories, for example, Rummel's theory is not 'formal'. 'The … theory presented here', Rummel (1979: 211) observes, '… is a comprehensive perspective involving hard theory (equations and explicit logic) integrated within a philosophical, metasocial and intuitive framework.' Even though Rummel's approach is not reducible to an 'axiomatic system', he does provide 33 propositions on conflict that are closely inter-related, and based on an extensively developed theoretical, as well as epistemological (even metaphysical) framework. A substantial portion of the theoretical and empirical work in the field of international relations today is either formal in nature, or when it moves beyond bivariate theoretical notions, has a tendency to bring in additional factors and hypotheses in a basically arbitrary (even if usually intuitively plausible) or ad hoc fashion. In UCW, Rummel may provide not only a valuable source of theoretical guidance and inspiration. Analysts who want to develop better theory, but are disinclined for whatever reason to rely on formal methods need an alternative. RJ Rummel's *Understanding Conflict and War* may provide such an alternative.

References

Benoit, Ken (1996) Democracies really are more pacific (in general): Reexamining regime type and war involvement. *Journal of Conflict Resolution* 40(4): 636–657.

Bremer, Stuart A (1992) Dangerous dyads: Conditions affecting the likelihood of interstate war, 1816–1965. *Journal of Conflict Resolution* 36(2): 309–341.

Bremer, Stuart A (1996) Power parity, political similarity, and capability concentration: Comparing three explanations of major power conflict. Paper presented at the 37th Annual Convention of the International Studies Association. San Diego, CA.

Bueno de Mesquita, Bruce & David Lalman (1992) *War and Reason*. New Haven, CT: Yale University Press.

Chan, Steve (1984) Mirror, mirror on the wall … Are freer countries more pacific? *Journal of Conflict Resolution* 28(4): 617–649.

Diehl, Paul (1985) Contiguity and military escalation in major power rivalries, 1816–1980. *Journal of Politics* 47(4): 1203–1211.

Doran, Charles F & Wes Parsons (1980) War and the cycle of relative power. *American Political Science Review* 74(4): 947–965.

Doyle, Michael (1983) Kant, liberal legacies, and foreign affairs. Parts I and II, *Philosophy and Public Affairs* 12(3): 205–235 and (4): 323–353.

East, Maurice & Philip M Gregg (1967) Factors influencing cooperation and conflict in the international system. *International Studies Quarterly* 11(3): 244–269.

Geller, Daniel (1985) *Domestic Factors in Foreign Policy*. Cambridge, MA: Schenckman.

Gartzke, Erik (2007) The capitalist peace. *American Journal of Political Science* 51(1): 166–191.

Gibler, Douglas M (2012) *The Territorial Peace: Borders, State Development, and International Conflict*. New York: Cambridge University Press.

Gilpin, Robert (1981) *War and Change in World Politics*. Cambridge: Cambridge University Press.

Gleditsch, Nils Petter (1992) Democracy and peace. *Journal of Peace Research* 29(4): 369–376.

Gochman, Charles S & Zeev Maoz (1984) Militarized interstate disputes, 1816–1976. *Journal of Conflict Resolution* 28(4): 585–616.

Goertz, Gary & Paul Diehl (1992) The empirical importance of enduring rivalries. *International Interactions* 18(2): 151–163.

Goertz, Gary & Paul Diehl (1993) Enduring rivalries: Theoretical constructs and empirical patterns. *International Studies Quarterly* 37(2): 147–171.

Goldstein, Joshua S (1988) *Long Cycles: Prosperity and War in the Modern Age*. New Haven, CT: Yale University Press.

Hensel, Paul (1994) One thing leads to another: Recurrent militarized disputes in Latin America, 1816–1986. *Journal of Peace Research* 31(3): 281–298.

Huth, Paul (1996) *Standing Your Ground: Territorial Disputes and International Conflict*. Ann Arbor, MI: University of Michigan Press.

Lave, Charles A & James G March (1975) *An Introduction to Models in the Social Sciences*. New York: Harper and Row.

Lemke, Douglas (1995) Small states and war: An expansion of power transition theory. In: Jacek Kugler & Douglas Lemke (eds) *Parity and War: Evaluations and Extensions of 'The War Ledger'*. Ann Arbor, MI: University of Michigan Press, 77–91.

Leng, Russell J (1993) *Interstate Crisis Behavior; 1816–1980: Realism vs. Reciprocity*. Cambridge: Cambridge University Press.

Leng, Russell J (1983) When will they ever learn: Coercive bargaining in recurrent crises. *Journal of Conflict Resolution* 27(3): 379–419.

Levy, Jack (1987) Declining power and the preventive motivation for war. *World Politics* 40(1): 82–107.

Levy, Jack (1988) Domestic politics and war. *Journal of Interdisciplinary History* 18(4): 653–673.

Maoz, Zeev (1990) *National Choices and International Processes*. Cambridge: Cambridge University Press.

Maoz, Zeev & Nasrin Abdolali (1989) Regime types and international conflict, 1817–1976. *Journal of Conflict Resolution* 33(1): 3–35.

Maoz, Zeev & Bruce Russett (1992) Alliance, contiguity, wealth, and political stability: Is the lack of conflict among democracies a statistical artifact? *International Interactions* 17(3): 245–267.

Maoz, Zeev & Bruce Russett (1993) Normative and structural causes of democratic peace, 1946–1986. *American Political Science Review* 87(3): 624–638.

Midlarsky, Manus (ed.) (1989) *Handbook of War Studies*. Boston, MA: Unwin Hyman.

Modelski, George (1978) The long cycle of global politics and the nation-state. *Comparative Studies in Society and History* 20(2): 214–235.

Morgan, T Clifton & Valerie Schwebach (1992) Take two democracies and call me in the morning: A prescription for peace? *International Interactions* 17(4): 305–320.

Mousseau, Michael (2013) The democratic peace unraveled: It's the economy. *International Studies Quarterly* 57(1): 186–197.

Oneal, John R & James Lee Ray (1997) New tests of the democratic peace: Controlling for economic interdependence, 1950–1985. *Political Research Quarterly* 50(4): 151–775.

Organski, AFK (1968) *World Politics*, 2nd ed. New York: Knopf.

Organski, AFK & Jacek Kugler (1980) *The War Ledger*. Chicago, IL: University of Chicago Press.

Pettersson, Therese & Peter Wallensteen (2015) Armed conflicts, 1946–2014. *Journal of Peace Research* 52(4): 536–550.

Ray, James Lee (1982) Understanding Rummel. *Journal of Conflict Resolution* 26(1): 161–187.

Ray, James Lee (1995) *Democracy and International Conflict*. Columbia, SC: University of South Carolina Press.

Ray, James Lee (1998) R J Rummel's Understanding Conflict and War: An overlooked classic? *Conflict Management and Peace Science* 16(2): 125–147.

Rousseau, David L; Christopher Gelpi, Dan Reiter & Paul K Huth (1996) Assessing the dyadic nature of the democratic peace, 1918–1988. *American Political Science Review* 90(3): 512–533.

Rummel, RJ (1970) *Applied Factor Analysis*. Evanston, IL: Northwestern University Press.

Rummel, RJ (1975–1981) Understanding Conflict and War, vols 1–5. Beverly Hills, CA: Sage.

Vol 1: *The Dynamic Psychological Field*, (1975).

Vol 2: *The Conflict Helix*, (1976).

Vol 3: *Conflict in Perspective*, (1977).

Vol 4: *War, Power, Peace*, (1979).

Vol 5: *The Just Peace*, (1981).

Rummel, RJ (1976) *Dimensions of Nations*. Beverly Hills, CA: Sage.

Rummel, RJ (1983) Libertarianism and international violence. *Journal of Conflict Resolution* 27(1): 27–71.

Rummel, RJ (1985) A test of libertarian propositions on violence within and between nations against published research results. *Journal of Conflict Resolution* 29(3): 419–455.

Rummel, RJ (1994) *Death by Government: Genocide and Mass Murder since 1900*. New Brunswick, NJ: Transaction.

Rummel, RJ (1995a) Democracy, power, genocide, and mass murder. *Journal of Conflict Resolution* 39(1): 3–26.

Rummel, RJ (1995b) Democracies ARE less warlike than other regimes. *European Journal of International Relations* 1(4): 457–479.

Russett, Bruce (1995) Processes of dyadic choice for war and peace. *World Politics* 47(2): 268–282.

Salmore, Stephen A & Charles G Hermann (1969) The effect of size, development, and accountability on foreign policy. *Peace Science Society Papers* 14(1): 16–30.

Sarkees, Meredith Reid & Frank Whelon Wayman (2010) *Resort to Arms, 1816–2007*. Washington, DC: CQ Press.

Schweller, Randall L (1992) Domestic structure and preventive war: Are democracies more
    pacific? *World Politics* 44(2): 235–269.
Spiro, David E (1994) The insignificance of the liberal peace. *International Security* 19(2): 50–86.
Thompson, William (1988) *On Global War*. Columbia, SC: University of South Carolina Press.
Vasquez, John (1993) *The War Puzzle*. Cambridge: Cambridge University Press.
Wallensteen, Peter (1981) Incompatibility, confrontation, and war: Four models and three
    historical systems, 1816–1976. *Journal of Peace Research* 18(1): 57–90.
Weede, Erich (1984) Democracy and war involvement. *Journal of Conflict Resolution* 28(4): 649–
    664.
Zinnes, Dina & Jonathan Wilkenfeld (1971) An analysis of foreign conflict behavior of nations. In:
    Wolfram F Hanrieder (ed.) *Comparing Foreign Policy*. New York: McKay (167–213).

Chapter 9
Rummel and Singer, DON and COW

Frank Whelon Wayman

When the scientific revolution in the study of international relations (IR) started in the 1960s, two prominent early pioneers who had particularly lasting impact on the field were Rudolph J. Rummel and J. David Singer.[1] Each led an enormous data project gathering information on sovereign states across the entire world over many decades, up to their time. Rummel's enterprise was the Dimensionality of Nations (DON) Project, while Singer's was the Correlates of War (COW) Project. This essay explains how the differences in these two projects have affected the study of world politics down to the present day. If so, in the future, the productivity of the field will depend in part on our understanding of the contrasting views of Rummel and Singer, which continue to affect what we are currently doing, and have implications for what we should do next.

To Rummel the regime (and, later, the pairing of regimes, or 'dyad') was the place to start in the study of warfare, genocide, and related mass killing, whereas to Singer the central point was the inter-state system in which various regimes (called state system members) were embedded.

Rummel's theoretical orientation, field theory, was similar to Singer's, general systems theory. Compared to most theories of the time (Dougherty & Pfaltzgraff, 1990), field and systems theory are relatively vague, providing a general orientation rather than predictions. This open architecture was part of the appeal of these frameworks to folks like Singer, who wanted empirically driven results rather than *a priori* pontification, and to develop datasets that were multi-theoretic in the sense

Frank Whelon Wayman, b. 1946, Ph.D. in political science (University of Pennsylvania, 1972), Professor of political science at University of Michigan-Dearborn. Recent co-authored books: *Predicting the Future in Science, Economics, and Politics* (Elgar, 2014), and *Resort to War* (CQ Press, 2010). Fields of interest: explanation and prediction of emerging global conditions; war, peace, and security; US national politics, especially public opinion, partisanship and presidential elections, and interest groups and the Congress; Email: fwayman@umich.edu.

[1]I would like to thank Nils Petter Gleditsch for important suggestions improving this chapter. I am also grateful to the two anonymous reviewers for their essential contributions.

© The Author(s) 2017
N.P. Gleditsch (ed.), *R.J. Rummel: An Assessment of His Many Contributions*,
SpringerBriefs on Pioneers in Science and Practice 37,
DOI 10.1007/978-3-319-54463-2_9

of being able to test warring hypotheses from different contending schools of IR. There are differences between system and field, in that a system has directed relations among its component parts, with feedback (e.g., A attacks B, B defeats A, B changes the system, establishing an international organization to try to prevent attacks; or A attacks B because of a certain systemic power distribution, then war changes the power distribution, affecting the probability of subsequent wars), whereas in field theory there usually is not such a 'cybernetic' set of relationships and feedback loops. Instead, in a force field, there can be continuous pair-wise repulsion or attraction.

As explained in his five-volume study, *Understanding Conflict and War*, Rummel (1975) organized his thinking around a certain type of field theory. In practice, fields involve variables whose associations or correlations have an angular expression, which leads to Rummel's (1970) most widely-cited publication, *Applied Factor Analysis*, about a statistical tool for determining the number of dimensions in a space we need to study, and telling us the coordinates of the variables and cases in the resulting or 'reduced' space. A field can be a geographic grid, such as a farmer's field or the longitudes and latitudes of Earth; an abstract, mathematical expression of this, such as the Cartesian coordinates; or a force field in such a spatial array, in which forces acting at a distance, such as electromagnetism or gravity, pull objects around. Rummel (1975) distinguishes 'a region of space' from 'the area in which a force operates', and says the former undergirds spatial theory, the latter, field theory. He is concerned with 'intentional' fields that one would find in psychological and social work (the latter including Wright, 1955).

This orientation became central to Rummel's DON project. Rummel earned his Ph.D. at Northwestern University, where he developed DON for his dissertation while under the tutelage of Harold Guetzkow, one of the pioneers in the behavioral revolution in international relations. Guetkow was searching for cross-national data for his Inter-Nation Simulation, and this led him to imagine what became the DON Project. In that crucible, 'the earliest event-data project of major proportions began in 1962 … [when] Rummel assembled data … originally for use in Harold Guetzkow's Inter-Nation Simulation' (Merritt, Muncaster & Zinnes, 1993: 4). By contrast, Singer's COW Project, launched the next year, was Singer's own idea from the outset, and as such would become a more central and hence more persistent part of Singer's professional identity and life work.

After Rummel had dealt with missing data by an iterative process—beginning with variables that had little missing data, and then gradually filling in estimates of values for the other variables, a phase one of the project emerged, with nations placed in a multidimensional space of numbered factors. There was a lack of association between domestic instability and foreign conflict. At the start of his career, however, Rummel (1966) indicated where he was going with this null finding; his words anticipated DON's phase two, the dyadic studies:

Foreign conflict behavior is not internally derived. Its genesis lies outside the nation. It is a relational phenomenon depending on the degree of economic, social, and political similarity between nations. … Whether conflict actually occurs depends in part on the social and value distances between the nations.

Rummel's example is dyadic: 'Even nations that participate very little in the international system may have great conflict with each other if they are contiguous while having a great social and value distance between them (e.g. Israel and Syria)'. Staying this course of looking at dyadic relations, Rummel (1983) eventually published the law that followed from it, the inter-democratic peace.

At Rummel's website, the dominant theme is that power kills (http://www. hawaii.edu/powerkills/). As he began one of his books (Rummel, 1994: 1), 'Power kills; absolute power kills absolutely. This new Power Principle is the message emerging from my previous work on the causes of war and from this work on genocide and government mass murder … The more power a government has, the more it can act arbitrarily.'

A major supporting idea is the term regime, as operationalized by Rummel (1995) and used as the organizing principle for his datasets on 'democide—genocide and mass murder' (Rummel, 1998: 1). This idea of a regime is important to his work because there is a lot of variation from regime to regime in the regime's amount of power, and also in the number of people the regime kills. And Rummel's dominant theme is that those two characteristics of a regime (power and deaths) co-vary. In my own ordinary language, a regime is a type of government controlling a state apparatus. As Rummel (1995: 9) says, 'The changes from the Kaiser monarchy to the Weimar Republic to Hitler's rule … give us three different German regimes. … I count 432 distinct state regimes during the period from 1900 to 1987'. Hence, there would be the czarist regime in Russia until 1917, and then the communist regime from 1917 to 1991. Between February and October 1917, there should I think be a transition period and transitional regime (under Kerensky). Individual rulers, such as general secretaries Stalin, Khrushchev, and Brezhnev, and their governments, do not represent distinct regimes of their own, but instead are all leaders, successively, of different administrations in the communist regime.

To me, Rummel's (1983) article made the first really convincing case for the inter-liberal or inter-democratic peace. I have since challenged thousands of people, from classrooms to conferences where I am speaking, to name any other proposition in the social sciences that is surprising or counter-intuitive, and that has (according to its advocates at least) no exceptions. No one has ever been able, in my presence, to name such a proposition—other than Rummel's.

The COW Project generated the data for the bulk of the hypothesis tests in IR for decades (Wayman & Singer, 1990: 247–248). And 'realist theory informed 90% of the hypotheses tested by IR scholars up to the 1970s' (Walker, 2013: 148). It was a bit of a shock that an anti-realist hypothesis, the inter-democratic peace, had produced such a paradigm-shattering result. Sadly, I never heard Singer say a good word about Rummel's studies confirming the inter-democratic peace hypothesis. Rummel had used COW data on wars, plus other people's data on democracy, Liberalism, and freedom of nations, to contradict one of Singer's claims (namely, Singer's contention that the inter-democratic peace was based on too few cases and too flawed in other ways to be taken to be true; Small & Singer, 1976). Deciphering

Singer's true position on this is complicated. When Geller & Singer (1998) pro-
duced a literature review of scientific studies of international conflict, while they did
caution that the evidence is 'not indisputable', they did acknowledge that 'the
evidence in the area of the joint freedom proposition is consistent and cumulative.
Democratic dyads are less likely to engage in war than are non-democratic pairs'
(Geller & Singer, 1998: 87–88). But on the other hand, on his own at his weekly
COW seminar, Singer was much more skeptical about the inter-democratic peace.
So it is not surprising that, four years after Geller & Singer's assessment, one of
Singer's students, Henderson (2002) wrote a book that constituted an attack on the
democratic peace literature. In the opening paragraph, Henderson says, 'It struck
me as strange that one of the doyen of the behavioral revolution would be such an
avid critic of what some scholars hail as the closest thing to an empirical law in the
field'.

Instead, Singer seemed more interested in the international or interstate system.
While Waltz (1979: 94) defined 'international political structures in terms of states',
Singer spoke of 'the national state as level of analysis' (Singer, 1961: 82–89). Thus,
whereas Waltz writes of a system whose basic units are sovereign states, Singer
ends up with two systems: an inter-state system and an international system. The
international system consists of entities that have an international political goal
(including … state creation or survival), engage in international political behavior
(including inter-state or extra-state conflict, alliances, trade, or international organizations), or engage in political behavior that has international consequences (such
as civil wars). The [international] system … includes … terrorist groups (Sarkees &
Wayman, 2010: 27).

Nested within this international system is the interstate system, beginning in
1816, distinguished in terms of 'recurring international interactions between and
among the interstate system members' (Sarkees & Wayman, 2010: 16). Singer's
COW data are organized around a focus on state system membership. Basically,
between 1816 and 1919 an entity is a state system member if it has 500,000 people
or more and is diplomatically recognized at an adequate level by Britain and France,
while after 1919 it is a state if it is a League of Nations or UN member or has
500,000 people and diplomatic recognition by two major powers. (Note that 'state'
becomes a short-hand for 'state system member'; Bremer & Ghosn, 2003.)

Much confusion results from the short-hand expressions 'state' and 'system'.
'Whenever the word "system" was used without a modifier, Singer & Small were
referring to the interstate system' (Sarkees & Wayman, 2010: 16). Likewise, the
'states' whose characteristics are listed in the COW datasets are not the population
of states, but the population of state system members.

Singer's most widely-cited explanatory articles on interstate war are probably
Deutsch & Singer (1964) and Singer, Bremer & Stuckey (1972). Both operate at the
system level of analysis. It may be that Singer's devotion to the interstate system is
part of what made him reluctant to embrace the inter-democratic peace. As he said
in another widely-cited article, the international system level of analysis 'almost
inevitably requires that we postulate a high degree of uniformity in the foreign
policy codes of our national actors', and 'the system-oriented approach tends to

produce a sort of "black box" or "billiard ball" concept of national actors'. This is consistent with his foreign policy instincts, which were loath to attribute 'white hats' to the 'free world' and 'black hats' to the Soviet Union, in the assigning of blame for the dangers to world peace in the Cold War era. Singer's posture was very different from Rummel's, with Rummel in favor of Reagan's foreign policy and against détente. In these Cold War contexts, Singer may have been uncomfortable with Rummel's summary that 'freedom preserves peace and life'.

Singer wrote 'it is evident that my research and teaching has unambiguously been problem-driven', and 'for reasons that I struggle to articulate, the problem has been, and remains, that of war' (Singer, 1990: 2). The COW Project was founded by him at the University of Michigan in 1963, the year after the world nearly was destroyed, had the Cuban Missiles Crisis gone badly. International war attracted Singer's best efforts at finding the 'causes of war and conditions of peace' (1990: 3). As he and Small put it, their focus is a 'preoccupation with the elimination of international war and the possible role of solid explanatory knowledge in that enterprise' (Small & Singer, 1982: 17). The first COW war handbook, *Wages of War* (Singer & Small, 1972) was consequently limited to international wars. Karl Deutsch subsequently convinced Singer that there was a need for a comparable list of civil wars. This led to a new handbook, *Resort to Arms: International and Civil Wars, 1816–1980*, presenting a 'comprehensive list that will enhance ... study of civil wars' (Small & Singer, 1982: 204). The civil war list is accompanied with a cautionary note, 'International war remains our major concern ... A research assault on [explanation of] civil war ... is clearly a task better left to others' (Small & Singer, 1982: 17). Consequently, the COW project had many datasets (such as the Militarized Interstate Dispute dataset) on the correlates of interstate war, but nothing comparable on the civil war data. Nevertheless, the publication of the civil war data was a valuable contribution to studies of civil war, and was also a step toward the full delineation of the totality of modern war. This was followed, in the third COW handbook (Sarkees & Wayman, 2010) with a definition and list of non-state wars, completing the full reckoning of the patterns of war in the past two centuries. Also, the focus of Singer on international war was somewhat vindicated by his co-authored article revealing that, over the time since the Congress of Vienna, inter-state wars had resulted in 32 million battle deaths, intra-state wars only 18 million (Sarkees, Wayman & Singer, 2003).

Critics often ask if the COW project has a state-centric bias. A more subtle and I think effective line of inquiry is to ask why the COW project has emphasized state-system-membership rather than simple sovereignty and independence as the defining characteristic of the state. This can cause confusion. For example, a number of non-state wars, including the main phase of one of the deadliest wars in history, the Taiping Rebellion, have been fought in areas that would be considered to be states by students of comparative politics. This and other related difficulties have led pioneers outside the COW project (Gleditsch, 2004; Fazal, 2007), as well as Singer's successor at the COW Project (Bremer & Ghosn, 2003) to propose various revisions and expansions of the concept of the state, to go beyond the COW state membership definition. These difficulties and challenges continue to provide important frontiers for research on war and the state in coming years.

In contrast to Singer, Rummel seems to me to have taken a more inductivist, practical approach to states and similar entities. On his website, powerkills.com, one finds a focus on killing, even of one person. The perpetrators are often leaders of totalitarian states, such as Mao, but can also be rebel leaders (the young Mao) or a king (Leopold of Belgium) who controls what some call a colony (the Belgian Congo) but Rummel calls Leopold's personal property. The unit of analysis becomes the regime and regime-like power-centers such as Leopold's Congo or Mao's rebel territory.

Rummel (1986) concluded that 'War isn't this century's biggest killer'. As he said then, 'About 35,654,000 people have died in this century's international and domestic wars, revolutions, and violent conflicts. … The number of people killed by totalitarian or extreme authoritarian governments already far exceeds that for all wars, civil and international. Indeed, this number already approximates the number that might be killed in a nuclear war'. He itemized 95 million killed by communist governments, but only '831,000 killed by free democratic governments'. Those killed by free democratic governments were always foreigners:

In no case have I found a democratic government carrying out massacres, genocide and mass executions of its own citizens … Absolutist governments (those that Freedom House would classify as not free) are not only many times deadlier than war, but are themselves the major factor causing war and other forms of violent conflict. They are a major cause of militarism. Indeed, absolutism, not war, is mankind's deadliest scourge of all. In light of all this, the peaceful, nonviolent fostering of civil liberties and political rights must be made mankind's highest humanitarian goal … because freedom preserves peace and life (Rummel, 1986).

A foundational premise of the COW Project was well expressed by Singer's student, Paul F Diehl, in the opening line of his Presidential address at ISA: 'War is the most important subject matter you can study',[2] because of the hundreds of millions dead in modern war and the trillions of dollars spent on the military every year. It was a shock to COW then when Rummel (1986) asserted that, in the catalogue of carnage carried out by modern humans against their own species, war wasn't the biggest killer. I agree it is more useful than usually realized to emulate Rummel and study both war and the slaughter of the innocents with the totality of such carnage in mind.

We certainly could use more work on the regime, a form of government with a temporal extent in-between the long-enduring state and the evanescent individual administration. It would be great to have a Rummel-inspired mutually exclusive and exhaustive list of regimes; and useful to have more refinements of Rummel's data on regimes and democide. Very constructively, Rolseth, Gleditsch & Theisen (2015) have built a nation-year version of Rummel's democide data. When Tago and I, in the footsteps of Rummel and Harff, created our own nation-year dataset on

---

[2]For a revised version, see Diehl (2016: 1).

wars, genocides, and political characteristics of nations (Wayman & Tago, 2004, 2010), we pored over Rummel's valuable *Statistics of Democide* (Rummel, 1998). We have entries from Rummel 1998—e.g., for Japan 1937–45, Japanese war dead 2,521,000 (Rummel, 1998: 39), and 5,964,000 democide (Rummel, 1998: 46–47). We can divide them by the number of years (nine in this case), and arrive at a genocide and mass murder total of 662,667 per year. This would be true of COW data on a war, too—think of World War I—but it is a little trickier for Rummel. These data are often aggregated in Rummel (1998) into totals by regime, and, for instance, the USSR regime lasts from 1917 to the end of his dataset in 1987, and so it is time-consuming at best to break out the effects in different years (how many died, e.g., in 1954?) and by government (e.g., Stalin vs. Khrushchev). One could compare what Tago and I did with the Rolseth, Theisen & Gleditsch data, and then see if the benefits of more refinements would warrant the costs.

When the first survey of IR scholars was done by *Foreign Policy* magazine, to assess who was most influential in their midst (Peterson, Tierney & Maliniak, 2005), Rummel did not make the top twenty-five thinkers; Singer did. Citations to their work produce similar results—Rummel a tad behind Singer. Realism, often claiming separation of domestic and international politics, was the only paradigm with more than one person in that top five. Nothing could be more destructive of this realist claim than Rummel's work on regimes, which shows that regime type matters (Wayman & Diehl, 1994). It is heartening to me that two people who continued Rummel's investigation of the inter-democratic peace, Bruce Russett and Michael Doyle, did make the list of the top IR scholars. Apparently, evidence was making some headway in undermining old paradigms. This makes me recall the prediction of Anatol Rapoport, on the trajectory of the COW Project as it was being launched in 1963. Rapoport said to David Singer 'we were not likely to come up with an integrated explanatory theory of war, ... but at least we would lay to rest many of the foolish platitudes that had ... led too many nations into the brutal abyss of war' (Singer paraphrasing Rapoport, in Sarkees & Wayman, 2010: xiii). The progress described in this essay, the progress of Rummel's doing, was based on the opposite of realism on this point, namely, his insisting on the unity of the study of international and domestic politics, including an examination of the role of regime type in mass violence—both democide and the inter-democratic peace.

When he took over from Singer as COW Director, Stuart Bremer convened a conference at Penn State University, on 'Future Wars and the Future Study of War'. Bremer's keynote address (Bremer & Ghosn, 2003) focused on whether the COW definition of state was too restrictive, and proposed measuring two dimensions of statehood, autonomy (stamps, money, military forces, autonomous foreign policy, size of territory and of population) and recognition (treaties, diplomatic recognition, participation in international conferences and in IGOs)—more as continuous variables than dichotomies. If done by COW, would this Herculean endeavor not make COW a 'DON' project?

The non-state wars list of Sarkees & Wayman (2010) has hopefully been a helpful move in expanding our understanding of armed conflict beyond system members, but, just to take one example from that book, a list of all sovereign states would help us divide the newly listed non-state wars into those internal to and those external to a given autonomous state.

The 21st century differs from the 20th. There have been no inter-state war onsets since the US invasion of Iraq in 2003. The twelve-year gap is the longest since the 18-year lull of 1828–1846. There are 25 war onsets since the end of 2007, for 3.33 onsets per year. That's the same pace as in Sarkees & Wayman (2010), which records 3.41 per year. The 25 recent wars are mostly intra-state. Democide is most closely correlated with intra-state war, less associated with extra-state war, and least associated with inter-state war (Wayman & Tago, 2010: 13). So far in the 21st century then, we have intra-state wars, causing great harm to civilian populations. The totalitarianism of the Nazis, Stalin, and Mao largely passed from the scene even before the end of the Cold War. War and death of the innocents continue, but not exactly as in the day of Rummel and Singer. With warfare now more civil, and the civilian deaths less from communist gulags, and more connected to insurgent and counter-guerrilla fighting, it seems that the tide has swung more around to the views of Harff & Gurr (1988) and Harff (2003). Harff warned that 'geno-politicide' was continuing at an alarming rate, and was predictable from a set of six variables—e.g., authoritarian regimes, but also civil war and lack of openness to international trade. While it would be great to have Rummel's democide data updated from 1987 (when he retired it), in the meantime we are well-served by war data and Harff's geno-politicide data, both of which fit well into the post-Cold-War narrative of civil war and geno-politicide.

As one indication of the enduring legacy of Rummel and Singer, in the judgment of Moore (1995), first director of the US Institute of Peace, the greatest advances in the study of war and peace included (1) Wright's pioneering organization of the field, *A Study of War*; (2) the project that Wright inspired, COW; (3) the recognition of the human, governmental, and international systemic levels of analysis through the impact of Waltz's *Man, the State, and War*; and (4) the discovery of the first powerful and surprising regularity in the field, the proposition of the inter-democratic peace, by Rummel. Shakespeare wrote, 'The evil that men do lives after them. The good is oft interred with their bones'. Oft interred, but not always. Further good will yet come, I think, from Singer's and Rummel's work.

References

Bremer, Stuart & Faten Ghosn (2003) Defining states. *Conflict Management and Peace Science* 20(1): 21–41.

Deutsch, Karl & J David Singer (1964) Multipolar systems and international stability. *World Politics* 16(3): 390–406.

Diehl, Paul F (2016) Exploring peace: Looking beyond war and negative peace. Presidential address, International Studies Association. *International Studies Quarterly* 60(1): 1–10.

Dougherty, James E & Robert L Pfaltzgraff (1990) *Contending Theories of International Relations: A Comprehensive Survey*. New York: Harper & Row.

Fazal, Tanisha (2007) *State Death*. Princeton, NJ: Princeton University Press.

Geller, Daniel S & J David Singer (1998) *Nations at War*. Cambridge: Cambridge University Press.

Gleditsch, Kristian (2004) A revised list of wars between and within independent states, 1816–2002. *International Interactions* 30(3): 231–262.

Harff, Barbara (2003) No lessons learned from the holocaust? Assessing risks of genocide and mass murder since 1955. *American Political Science Review* 97(1): 57–74.

Harff, Barbara & Ted Robert Gurr (1988) Toward empirical theory of genocides and politicides: Identification and measurement of cases since 1945. *International Studies Quarterly* 32(3): 359–371.

Henderson, Errol (2002) *Democracy and War: The End of an Illusion?* Boulder, CO: Lynne Rienner.

Moore, John (1995) Remarks in honor of RJ Rummel. Presented at the 36th Annual Convention of the International Studies Association, Chicago, IL, 21–25 February.

Merritt, Richard L; Robert G Muncaster & Dina Zinnes (1993) *International Event-Data Developments*. Ann Arbor, MI: University of Michigan Press.

Peterson, Susan; Michael J Tierney & Daniel Maliniak (2005) Inside the ivory tower. *Foreign Policy* November/December: 58–65.

Rolseth, Amund; Nils Petter Gleditsch & Ole Magnus Theisen (2015) Violence against civilians, 1900–1987. Paper presented at the 57th Annual Convention of the International Studies Association, New Orleans, LA, 18–21 February.

Rummel, Rudolph J (1966) Some dimensions in the foreign behavior of nations. *Journal of Peace Research* 3(3): 201–223.

Rummel, Rudolph J (1970) *Applied Factor Analysis*. Evanston, IL: Northwestern University Press.

Rummel, Rudolph J (1975, 1976, 1977, 1979, 1981) *Understanding Conflict and War*. Beverly Hills, CA: Sage.

Rummel, Rudolph J (1983) Libertarianism and international violence. *Journal of Conflict Resolution*, 27(1): 27–71.

Rummel, Rudolph J (1986) War isn't this century's biggest killer. *Wall Street Journal*, 7 July.

Rummel, Rudolph J (1994) *Death by Government*. New Brunswick, NJ: Transaction.

Rummel, Rudolph J (1995) Democracy, power, genocide, and mass murder. *Journal of Conflict Resolution* 39(1): 3–26.

Rummel, Rudolph J (1998) *Statistics of Democide: Genocide and Mass Murder since 1900*. Munster: Lit Verlag.

Sarkees, Meredith Reid & Frank Whelon Wayman (2010) *Resort to War: A Data Guide to Inter-state, Extra-state, Intra-state, and Non-state Wars, 1816–2007*. Washington, DC: CQ Press.

Sarkees, Meredith Reid; Frank Whelon Wayman & J David Singer (2003) Inter-state, intra-state, and extra-state wars: A comprehensive look at their distribution over time, 1816–1997. *International Studies Quarterly* 47(1): 49–70.

Singer, J David (1961) The level of analysis problem in international relations. In: Klaus Knorr & Sidney Verba (eds) *The International System: Theoretical Essays*. Princeton, NJ: Princeton University Press, 77–92.

Singer, J David (1990) *Models, Methods, and Progress in World Politics: A Peace Research Odyssey*. Boulder, CO: Westview.

Singer, J David; Stuart Bremer & John Stuckey (1972) Capability distribution, uncertainty, and major power war, 1820–1965. In: Bruce Russett (ed.) *Peace, War, and Numbers*. Beverly Hills, CA: Sage, 19–48.

Small, Melvin & J David Singer (1976) The war proneness of democratic regimes, 1816–1965. *Jerusalem Journal of International Relations* 1(1): 49–69.

Small, Melvin & J David Singer (1982) *Resort to Arms: International and Civil Wars, 1816–1980*. Beverley Hills, CA: Sage.

Walker, Thomas (2013) A circumspect revival of liberalism: Robert O Keohane and Joseph S Nye's Power and Interdependence. In: Henrik Bliddal et al. (eds) *Classics of International Relations*. Hoboken, NJ: Taylor & Francis, 148–156.

Waltz, Kenneth (1959) *Man, the State, and War*. New York: Columbia University Press.

Waltz, Kenneth (1979) *Theory of International Politics*. Reading, MA: Addison-Wesley.

Wayman, Frank Whelon & Paul F Diehl (1994) *Reconstructing Realpolitik*. Ann Arbor, MI: University of Michigan Press.

Wayman, Frank Whelon & J David Singer (1990) Evolution and directions for improvement in the Correlates of War Project methodologies. In: J David Singer & Paul F Diehl (eds) *Measuring the Correlates of War*. Ann Arbor, MI: University of Michigan Press, 247–267.

Wayman, Frank W & Atsushi Tago (2004) Predicting crimes against humanity: Effects of war, democracy, economic development, and UN intervention, 1946–2000. Paper presented at the 45th Annual Convention of the International Studies Association, Montréal, Québec, 17–20 March.

Wayman, Frank W & Atsushi Tago (2010) Explaining the onset of mass killing, 1949–87. *Journal of Peace Research* 47(1): 3–14.

Wright, Quincy (1942) *A Study of War*. Chicago, IL: University of Chicago Press.

Wright, Quincy (1955) *The Study of International Relations*. New York: Appleton-Century-Crofts.

Chapter 10
Regime Type Matters

H.-C. Peterson

10.1 Introduction

Rummel's pioneering work is giving us a revolutionary, practical solution to violence between states (war) and between people and state (democide): democracy. He finds 'regime type' (kind of government) to be one of the strongest explanations for war and democide because it deals with restraining government power. The solution is revolutionary because it challenges existing ways of looking at the world, and practical because it is within the capability of states and the international system to accomplish.

Here is Rummel (2005a) on how regime type matters:

> I do believe that some governments are better than others; that the current German government is morally superior to Hitler's, contemporary Russia's to Stalin's, and Japan's to its militarist government of World War II. Indeed, I believe that the government that best promotes the development of its people in terms of their own interests and capabilities, while minimizing internal and foreign violence and democide, as does democracy, is better than those that don't. This is my prejudice and sense of social justice.

This regime-based approach is superficially known as 'no wars between democracies,' but not yet fully grasped. This despite Russett (1993: 138), who closes with 'But if the chance for wider democratization can be grasped and consolidated, international politics might be transformed,' and 'A system created by autocracies centuries ago might now be recreated by a critical mass of democratic states.' These two 'might' statements have not yet transformed international politics nor recreated the international system, and the democratic peace remains in limbo.

H.-C. Pete (Peterson), Jr., b. 1951, Ph.D. in Political Science (University of Hawaii, 2001); US Marine Corps 1973–93; Lecturer, Department of Political Science & International Relations, University of San Diego (2003–); Adjunct Instructor, Political Science, San Diego Mesa College (2002–). Teaching interests: international relations in the 21st Century, geopolitics, genocide and democide, and democracy and peace. Email: polsciprof@sbcglobal.net.

© The Author(s) 2017   91
N.P. Gleditsch (ed.), *R.J. Rummel: An Assessment of His Many Contributions*,
SpringerBriefs on Pioneers in Science and Practice 37,
DOI 10.1007/978-3-319-54463-2_10

Rummel's work is an integrated worldview: its foundation is that the kind of government is of utmost importance to its own citizens (will our government kill us?) and other countries (will there be war?), so Rummel can by synthesized: regime type matters. This bridges the empirical democratic peace with a powerful prescription: if you want peace, and life, you must choose the regime type that protects it best: democracy.

From this worldview comes one general principle, that democracy is a powerful and reliable method of nonviolence, and five associated propositions, best set forth in Rummel (1997): first, a pair of democracies do not make war on each other; second, the more democratic any two countries, the less their bilateral violence; and third, the more democratic a country, the fewer its own casualties in war. These are about international relations. The fourth is internal: the more democratic a country, the less internal political violence. Finally, the more democratic a country, the less its democide.

Ending war and mass murder, and building positive peace, are the highest goals of secular life, and because Rummel offers empirically valid, theoretically sound, practical solutions to that end, I view Rummel as one of the most important thinkers of the 20th century.

To understand this I have found Chadwick's (2006) Goal-Drift-Actual framework invaluable. The GDA model centers on science, philosophy, and praxis, integrating political science (the empirical, what we know), political philosophy (theory, our understanding and convictions), and political action (what we do). The GDA is a powerful alternative to Johan Galtung's Diagnosis-Prognosis-Therapy (DPT) model, which treats human interactions as illnesses to be cured. The GDA is less arrogant, lacking the DPTs presumptive privilege of the analyst as wise doctor, and from a power-limiting, freedom-favoring perspective, the GDA is a preferred model.

Using the GDA to look at Rummel's work we find extensive political science in his robust empirical work that was essential to establish the democratic peace. There is highly developed political philosophy, from the 'the conflict helix' (Rummel, 1991), to the three levels of explanation for democracy as a method of nonviolence (Rummel, 1997). Regarding praxis, Rummel argues that because of the science of the democratic peace, and the conviction that democracy reliably reduces violence, there is an imperative to 'foster freedom.' This integration, linked by regime type, offers a transformative politics, transcending realism and liberalism, while negating neither. For Rummel, realism must understand that democracies behave differently, and liberalism must understand that peace is best achieved among democracies.

10.2   Rummel's Regime Type Matters Trajectory—From DON to BBF

Throughout his career Rummel tried to answer 'what gives my life meaning?' He explains (Rummel, 1997: ix): 'My true interest was in understanding and doing something about the legal killing called war' and 'this has been my ultimate concern.' Later he was 'shocked to discover that several times more people were killed in democide (genocide and mass murder) by governments than died in warfare.' War and democide, the two most lethal of human interactions, have been Rummel's lifetime work. From Rummel's first book in 1975 to his last in 2007, every book, article, chapter, monograph, chart, novel, docudrama, and blog commentary supports the fact that the kind of government countries have has enormous consequences: life or death, peace or war. This connects everything in Rummel's life's work, which is an unfolding discovery of how and why regime differences are important, from the initial glimmers of the DON, to the democratic peace, then democide, and finally positive peace. This trajectory can be traced in his major works, culminating in his call for an alliance of democracies.

Early in his career, he was the prime mover of the Dimensionality of Nations (DON) Project, which was the foundation for his analysis of regime type, done in *Understanding Conflict and War* (1975–81). Next, he zeroed in on the democratic peace with three groundbreaking articles (Rummel, 1983, 1984, 1985) that became the first four propositions. Democide was added in 1986 with 'War isn't this century's biggest killer,' becoming the fifth proposition.

Democide research continued with four books documenting the over ten million each killed by the Soviet Union, both Communist and Nationalist Chinese regimes, and Nazi Germany. *Death by Government* (1994), his best known and best-selling book (apart from the one on factor analysis), defined democide more rigorously, and presented empirical work in 15 case studies. Finally, *Statistics of Democide* (1998) contains all the data linking specific regimes to democide, with extensive exposition; this is the only resource I have found specifically including US democide.

In 1997 Rummel presented his grand summary, *Power Kills: Democracy as A Method of Nonviolence*. It reads easily, and is organized simply: 5–3–3. The five propositions cover a wide range of empirical relationships between regime type and violence; there are three regime types (democratic, authoritarian, and totalitarian); and three levels of theory explain why democracy reduces violence. This is the single best work on the democratic peace, integrating empirical evidence with well-argued theory. Every graph of regime type and violence shows the same: more democracy, less violence.

Retiring in 1995, Rummel did updates and current analysis. A reticent speaker, and losing his hearing, he communicated mostly on the internet, publishing extensively on his website, Power Kills. This remains the single most important Rummel resource, containing most of his books, many stand-alone articles, over 500 blog posts, six alternative history novels based on his work, an update on his democide estimates for the 20th century (from 174 million to 262 million), and an extensive Democratic Peace Q&A (Rummel, 2005a).

Rummel's last book was *The Blue Book of Freedom: Ending Famine, Poverty, Democide and War* (2007), a decade after *Power Kills*. This non-academic, but well documented book shows how much Rummel added to the original democratic peace, arguing that democracy not only reduced violence, but made for better life. This was an important expansion of his work, much less appreciated than the conventional democratic peace. Two tables are illustrative (Rummel, 2007: 62, 116, also in Rummel, 2005b: 224): one on 'surviving': democracies experience the least war, international violence, internal violence, and democide; the other on 'thriving': democracies have the highest levels of human development, and the lowest levels of poverty. Reinforcing the importance of regime type, he made a plea for the freedom that democracy protects (2007: 117): 'Freedom is every person's right. And it is a moral good in that it promotes wealth, prosperity, social justice, and nonviolence, and it preserves human life.'

Although many may disagree, if he was correct about his work also connecting democracy with positive peace by means of asserting that regime type is so critical, then his work will become more widely known, understood, and acted on, and he will be recognized as the grand thinker I believe he was.

10.3   An Assessment

What has become of Rummel's work? For perspective, consider this prediction (Gleditsch, 1992: 372):

> ... the perfect or near-perfect correlation between democracy and nonwar in dyads should soon begin to have a very different effect: all research on the causes of war in modern times will be regarded as suspect if it is not corrected for this factor. In fact, I would argue that most behavioral research on conditions for war and peace in the modern world can now be throw on the scrap-heap of history, and researchers can start again on a new basis.

What happened? Despite extensive democratic peace research during the 1990s, not much. The 'no wars between democracies' proposition has indeed become widely accepted in international relations, but remains curiously unimportant, even disparaged as an excuse to do forcible regime change (Russett, 2005, 2008). The other propositions are largely absent, regime type is not routinely included in studies of war and peace, and has not permeated standard models of international relations. Realism doesn't like democracy, preferring 'stability'; liberalism doesn't want anything to do with regime change. And democide is largely disconnected from the democratic peace. Regime type is not a significant part of academic or policy-related international relations.

10.4   Academics

Scholarly research continues on the democratic peace, mostly about internal nuances such as the relative strength of various factors, and the addition to regime type of trade and international organizations (Russett & Oneal, 2001) which revives and modernizes Kant's *Perpetual Peace*. Rummel supported such research, but saw it as ancillary to the 'prime directive' that democracy, as a regime type, best limits violence. Yet the discipline fragments rather than integrates the democratic peace, which has certainly not achieved paradigm status.

One way to see this is in textbooks, reflecting the state of a discipline. Although I have taught international relations for over a decade, it has been hard to find one that makes more than a passing reference to the peace among democracies, much less the larger issue of democracy as a method of nonviolence. A notable exception was Russett, Starr & Kinsella (2010), although subsequent editions have less democratic peace emphasis. Democide, responsible for over 260 million deaths in the 20th century (far more than war deaths), is consistently absent, at best getting a short paragraph. This is true even in the genocide literature. For example, Totten & Bartop (2009), a thorough presentation of genocide studies, is almost completely democide-free: the index has only one mention of Rummel, and one of democide.

10.5   Policy

Have Rummel's propositions transformed international relations? US foreign policy shows little evidence. President Barack Obama was agnostic about regime type mattering, much less about democracy promotion. This is understandable given the assertive foreign policy (Russett, Starr & Kinsella, 2010: 102 call it 'offensive idealism') of President George W. Bush, who mentioned peace between democracies as one of several, but not the main, reasons for going to war against the regime of Saddam Hussein in Iraq in 2003. The consensus now is that if promoting democracy involves such wars, we shouldn't: in President Obama's words, 'don't do stupid stuff'. This is reflected (Clinton, 2009) in the '3D's' of Obama foreign policy: Defense, Diplomacy, and Development. But no Democracy. And no hint that regime type matters. Yet it does, and the refusal to assist the transition of Iraq in 2011 toward democracy will be an enduring case study of the consequences of ignoring regime type.

What about democide? The Obama administration ignored links between regime type and mass murder, and was not motivated to intervene to prevent democide, Syria being the best example. A possible exception was against the Muhamar Qaddafi regime in Libya in 2011, ostensibly to save Libyan lives. However, this fiasco may have been worse than Bush's deeply flawed regime change in Iraq (Diamond, 2005), because after regime destruction, nothing was done to effect democratic regime building, and violence and democide in Libya continue. Even having the great advocate for human rights, Samantha Power, as the US Ambassador to the UN since 2013 had not moved the US or the international community to actually do much about the proliferation of democides in the world. Perhaps the new UN doctrine of the Responsibility to Protect (R2P) will change this, although one can remain skeptical as it is not grounded in regime type.

In contrast, Rummel (2001) presented his most specific and ambitious proposal for what to do. His approach was regime based, arguing that since democracies do not war against each other, and democracies have virtually no democide, it is in the national interest of democracies to pursue democratization in order to avoid wars and humanitarian interventions. Since the UN has not aided democratization, an Alliance of Democracies should operate within the UN as a pro-democracy political party, and outside the UN to intervene to stop democides. This was a radical proposal, much more than the existing Community of Democracies, which Diamond (2008: 235) characterized as largely symbolic, forecasting it would 'gradually fade into insignificance.' Rummel's Alliance, in contrast, would escape the security dilemma (we fear and distrust others because they really might hurt us) by creating a security community, or zone of peace (no actual or expectation of violence) based on the pacifying effects of democracy. This was Rummel's praxis: democracies strengthening each other, especially newcomers, to effect sustained regime change in the world. But where is it?

My conclusion is that Rummel's work, while an extremely important contribution to politics, has not transformed it, nor become a new paradigm. Yet!

10.6   GDA-ing Rummel

The GDA helps understand why the democratic peace has not been transformative, and one might even conclude that it has failed in all three areas. Within political science, knowledge of the democratic peace is limited to the 'no wars between democracies' and perhaps the 'no democratic democicide' propositions. They exist as social science facts, but as mere acknowledgements. The other propositions are mostly unknown, and Rummel's bold statement (1997: 3) that we have a realistic solution to war, violence, and democicide remains ignored, contested, denied, or discarded.

Regarding political philosophy, few are grappling with why democracies are peaceful. Despite Rummel's three levels of explanation, a rich discourse on institutions and norms, and even the revived Kantian peace, agnosticism prevails. Academics are ambivalent, policy makers skeptical. Without understanding why the democratic peace is true and developing strong beliefs in its importance, it will remain a curiosity more than a motivation. If you don't believe in it, why commit to it?

Finally, in praxis, if knowledge and understanding are lacking, we cannot expect good action. The idea of regime changes toward democracy in order to achieve peace is a rejected project, absent from the declaratory and actual foreign policy of democracies.

10.7   Reflections on Rummel and Galtung

While a graduate student at Hawaii, I studied extensively with Rummel, and took his last classes. I also studied with a very different 'great thinker,' Johan Galtung. Both impressed me greatly, and influenced my thinking, although in very different ways.

My first day in class with Rummel, when he stated that democracies did not war against each other: 'this cannot be true … but what if it is?'

My first day in class with Galtung, as he set forth an exploration of six characteristics of five civilizations: 'wow, this is fascinating and very cool!'

Those impressions sum up my view of these two remarkable men. Galtung was a feast of new perspectives. He was great raconteur, and a joy to learn from. Nothing was irrelevant, and everything was viewed through a lens of peace: is it, or isn't it? Who could not be fascinated by fault lines, cosmologies, traumas, dialectics, civilizations, conflict life cycles, gender, culture, theses on development, inner and outer sectors of six kinds of spaces, and whatever else his broad epistemological mind-net could capture? This was a great adventure, but it was also easy: the only discipline was to try to fit everything into some semblance of inter-connected categories, and if you didn't like something, you could discard it. You did not need 'rigorous analysis:' anecdotes sufficed for evidence, profound comments for theory, and categories and charts for paradigm construction.

Listening to Galtung lecture was like lifting off in a rocket, the weighty g-forces of his intellect taking us far beyond the limits of earth's gravity, soaring into the omniscience of his own special gravitas, to boldly go where no social scientist had gone before. But soaring can also disconnect, and after a while, I saw Galtung as a master idea creator, using empirical terminology, but making bold assertions that were contradictory, confusing, and not well-grounded, particularly regarding democracy.

Rummel was exciting in a different way. Wars and regime types were not abstractions and were subjected to comprehensive rather than selective compilation, resolving rather than expanding debates over definitions (what is democracy?), and data were bounced off each other to see what would stick (did democracies ever fight each other?). Theories were constructed not to impress and astound, but to be disproved, and statistical analysis done to determine significance. Democide was morbidly fascinating, and morally exhausting, with the unbelievable numbers showing the prolific propensity for those with power to kill and kill and kill. But it all fit together. There was a unified theory explaining both wars and democide, and what kept it all together was power, connected by regime type. You could measure this with Freedom House (for regime type), the Correlates of War Project (for wars and violence), and Statistics of Democide. And you could do something about it: from Rummel's cautious 'foster freedom', to a global alliance of democracies.

Galtung and Rummel had little respect for each other. Galtung, profoundly of the left, saw Rummel as a war-mongering apologist for Imperial America. Rummel, a profoundly classical liberal, saw Galtung as a once-brilliant scholar drifting deeper into a freedom disparaging, US-hating left field. Rummel (1997: 113) recounts a 1988 Galtung memo alleging the CIA had killed six million people. This could not be misinterpreted, accusing the US of as much evil as Hitler's Holocaust of six million Jews. For Galtung, the democratic peace was impossible.

Galtung's *Peace by Peaceful Means* (1996) is the closest I can find of sustained engagement with the democratic peace, and shows deep misunderstanding. Galtung summarily dismissed 'democracies almost never fight each other' with 'I do not even believe in that one' (:58). No evidence needed, it is Galtung who says so. Instead, he developed nine theorems connecting democracy with vague 'belliger-ence.' But Galtung could not escape the realities of regime types, noting (:58) that 'Democratic rule is one of the greatest innovations of mankind.' Left unwritten is why. Or what he means by democracy, since (at least at the time I knew him) he believed that the Mao regime in China was an exemplar of what government should do. Galtung & Nishimura (1976) found six things we could learn from the Chinese, but not killing one's own citizens was not one of them. In a talk in Beijing (Galtung 2010) he said that China's image had been bad in the past because of 'certain excesses'. So much for the democide of 76 million Chinese. Even in 2015 he made the bizarre assertion that China was a model for positive peace, again overturning conventional political science. This was and is exciting stuff, but reflects an understanding of the world deeply at odds with Rummel's, ignoring the importance of regime type, and utterly dismissive of democide.

Another tempering of my fascination with him was during a class discussion about repression in North Korea, when Galtung said that he had visited the country, and all the people seemed happy, so reports of repression and killing were most likely Western fabrications. This comment from one of the core founders of peace studies was astonishing, and I realized that while Rummel's 'one big thing' was freedom and life, Galtung's was apparently the negation of the West.

Rummel found that regimes matter because of how they are limited from using power, something Galtung dismissed because I think he was neutral about power. To be hyper-critical of the West while ambivalent about communist regimes killing over 100 million people (Rummel, 1993) was about deeply incompatible world-views. There was no way Rummel and Galtung could follow the words of the prophet Isaiah to 'come let us reason together', even though both deeply desired the goal of that same Isaiah, that nations may 'beat their swords into plowshares.'

Their ideas will endure into the future, but I think Rummel's will prevail because he reminds us we must construct governments that cannot kill us, whereas Galtung's hundreds of ideas, much applauded on the peace and justice lecture circuit, will be scattered to the winds of unfolding history.

10.8   In Summary

Rummel sought an end of violence between and within states. His found empiri-cally that wars and democide occurred because governments with unchecked power commit much more violence than those with limits on their power, hence 'power kills.' He explained how and why democracy is a method of nonviolence, later adding that it reduces famine and poverty. This comprises the broad 'democratic peace.' The integrating link is that 'regime type matters.' Moving from science and philosophy to praxis, Rummel's prescription was to 'foster freedom', to nudge and change regimes toward democracy. Some aspects of the democratic peace are well accepted, but not the overall principle of democracy as a method of nonviolence which he called 'the most important fact of our time' (Rummel, 2007: 11, 21, 23). This has not captured the imagination of policy makers, nor generated policies to put the principle to work. Despite its achievements, this is the tragedy of the democratic peace.

What about the future of Rummel's work? I have two forecasts.

Optimistically, by mid-century (echoing Diamond, 2003) we will have near global democracy. A widespread realization will emerge that without more democracy, interstate violence will remain a constant threat to peace, and mass murders and genocides will continue. Based on this change in global consciousness —an enormous paradigm shift—there will be functional alliance of democracies to put the democratic peace into practice, and we will be on the way toward a Pax Democratica.

Pessimistically, democracy will still be a 'good thing,' and democratization will ebb and flow in the world. But because of the allure of power, and the difficulties in actually limiting it, there will still not be any widespread sense of urgency about fostering, nudging, or making pro-democracy regime changes. We will not realistically and reliably achieve what Rummel dreamed about: world peace, between nations and within them. Regime type will be ignored, war and democide will remain.

We shall see.

References

Chadwick, Richard W (2006) Reframing the meaning of democracy: The globalization of democratic development, viewed through the paradigms of political science, political practice, and political philosophy, http://www.hawaii.edu/intlrel/fukuoka2006_paper_97.pdf.

Clinton, Hillary, Secretary of State (2009) Testimony before the Senate Appropriations Committee, Washington, DC, 30 April, https://2009-2017.state.gov/secretary/20092013clinton/rm/2009a/04/122463.htm.

Diamond, Larry (2003) Universal democracy. *Policy Review* June/July, http://www.hoover.org/research/universal-democracy.

Diamond, Larry (2005) *Squandered Victory: The American Occupation and the Bungled Effort to Bring Democracy to Iraq*. New York: Holt.

Diamond, Larry (2008) *The Spirit of Democracy: The Struggle to Build Free Societies throughout the World*. New York: Holt.

Galtung, Johan (1996) *Peace by Peaceful Means: Peace and Conflict, Development, and Civilization*. London: Sage.

Galtung, Johan (2010) China ying/yang. TRANSCEND Media Service, 13 September, http://www.transcend.org/2010/09/china-yingyang/.

Galtung, Johan (2015) China vs. Russia vs. USA; Xi vs. Putin vs. Obama, TRANSCEND Media Service, 21 December, http://www.transcend.org/2015,12/china-vs-russia-vs-usa-xi-vs-putin-vs-obama/.

Galtung, Johan & Fumiko Nishimura (1976) Can we learn from the Chinese people? *World Development* 4(10–11): 883–888.

Gleditsch, Nils Petter (1992) Democracy and peace. *Journal of Peace Research* 29(4): 369–376.

Rummel, RJ (1975–1981) *Understanding Conflict and War*, 5 volumes. Beverly Hills, CA: Sage.

Rummel, RJ (1983) Libertarianism and international violence. *Journal of Conflict Resolution* 27(1): 27–71.

Rummel, RJ (1984) Libertarianism, violence within states, and the polarity principle. *Comparative Politics* 16(00): 443–462.

Rummel, RJ (1985) Libertarian propositions on violence within and between nations: A test against published results. *Journal of Conflict Resolution* 29(3): 419–455.

Rummel, RJ (1986) War isn't this century's biggest killer. *Wall Street Journal*, 7 July, http://www. hawaii.edu/powerkills/WSJ.ART.HTM.

Rummel, RJ (1991) *The Conflict Helix: Principles and Practices of Interpersonal, Social, and International Conflict and cooperation*. New Brunswick, NJ: Transaction.

Rummel, RJ (1993) How many did communist regimes murder?, http://www.hawaii.edu/ powerkills/COM.ART.HTM.

Rummel, RJ (1994) *Death by Government: Genocide and Mass Murder in the Twentieth Century*. New Brunswick, NJ: Transaction.

Rummel, RJ (1997) *Power Kills: Democracy as a Method of Nonviolence*. New Brunswick, NJ: Transaction.

Rummel, RJ (1998) *Statistics of Democide: Genocide and Mass Murder since 1900*. Munich: Lit Verlag.

Rummel, RJ (2001) Eliminating war and democide through an alliance of democracies. *International Journal of World Peace* 18(3): 55–68, http://www.hawaii.edu/powerkills/ ALLIANCE.HTM.

Rummel, RJ (2005a) Democratic peace Q&A version 2.0, http://www.hawaii.edu/powerkills/QA. V2.HTML.

Rummel, RJ (2005b) *Never Again Series Supplement*. Coral Springs, FL: Llumina.

Rummel, RJ (2007) *The Blue Book of Freedom*. Nashville, TN: Cumberland House.

Russett, Bruce (1993) *Grasping the Democratic Peace: Principles for a Post-Cold War World*. Princeton, NJ: Princeton University Press.

Russett, Bruce (2005) Bushwhacking the democratic peace. *International Studies Perspectives* 6 (4): 395–408.

Russett, Bruce & John R Oneal (2001) *Triangulating Peace: Democracy, Interdependence, and International Organizations*. New York: Norton.

Russett, Bruce; Harvey Starr & David Kinsella (2010) *World Politics: The Menu for Choice*, 9th ed. Boston, MA: Wadsworth.

Totten, Samuel & Paul R Bartop, eds (2009) *The Genocide Studies Reader*. New York: Routledge.

Chapter 11
Democracy as a Method of Nonviolence

Erica Chenoweth

In his seminal book *Power Kills*, Rummel (1997) summarizes decades of research on the democratic peace to make a single, pointed argument: that the worst kinds of violence—mass killings carried out by governments—are entirely explained by the tyrannical nature of the regime that commit such crimes.[1] His proposed solution to eliminating 'democide'—as well as collective violence, war initiation, and other forms of political violence—is a well-known known one: to promote and reinforce democratic government. His view is that strengthening democracy, both in terms of procedural practices and qualitative, liberal behavior—could result in world peace, defined as eliminating violence between states and within them. Rummel concludes that democracy is 'a method of nonviolence'—the subtitle of his book. In this chapter, I share some reflections on Rummel's basic argument, offering some observations, some critiques, and some paths forward for contemporary research on peace, democracy, and nonviolent change. In particular, I highlight one key deficit of Rummel's thesis: that he neglects the power of nonviolent civil resistance in bringing about democratization from below.

Erica Chenoweth, b. 1980, Ph.D. in political science (University of Colorado, 2007). She is now Professor and Associate Dean for Research at the Josef Korbel School of International Studies at the University of Denver and Associate Senior Researcher at the Peace Research Institute Oslo (PRIO). She has received several awards for her work, such as the Grawemeyer Award for Ideas Improving World Order (2013, with Maria J. Stephan) and the Karl Deutsch Award of the International Studies Association (2014); Email: Erica.chenoweth@du.edu.

[1]I thank Nils Petter Gleditsch, Doug Bond, and the panelists at the 56th Annual Convention of the International Studies Association, New Orleans, LA, 18–21 February 2015 for helpful comments and discussion. Any remaining mistakes are my own.

© The Author(s) 2017   101
N.P. Gleditsch (ed.), *R.J. Rummel: An Assessment of His Many Contributions*,
SpringerBriefs on Pioneers in Science and Practice 37,
DOI 10.1007/978-3-319-54463-2_11

11.1 Rummel's Motivation

What were Rummel's stated intentions in writing this book? He overtly expressed his normative goals. Although his study offers a sophisticated and detailed review of the empirical patterns of democracy, democide, war, and collective violence, he clearly lays out the primary source of his interest—to reduce war in all its forms while also elevating what he saw as the most practical and realistic method of political rule. In the preface, he writes:

'I hope to have something specific to recommend about ending war. But in the mid-1980s I was shocked to discover that several times more people were killed in democide (genocide and mass murder) by governments than died in warfare. And with that my aim broadened to help end or at least lessen this killing as well. This book presents the sum of all this research. And, I believe, I can finally offer what appears a most realistic and practical solution to war, democide, and other collective violence' (1997: ix).

Later, he writes: 'There is one solution to each and the solution in each case is the same. It is to foster democratic freedom and to democratize coercive power and force. That is, mass killing and mass murder carried out by government is a result of indiscriminate, irresponsible Power at the center' (ibid: 3).

What strikes the reader is the somewhat rare and refreshing statement about the author's own normative commitments—that of global emancipation as well as freedom from violence—motivating him to undertake the study. Such bold and self-revealing statements do not often appear at the outset of contemporary political science works, which are more typically characterized by the statement of an empirical puzzle, a correction to a theoretical framework, or the presentation of a new case. Here one sees an author who is not just interested in knowledge for its own sake, but who also wants to know how his academic discipline can bring its insights to bear on what he viewed as the most important questions of our time.

11.2 The Basic Argument

Rummel argues that democracy is indeed the most effective method by which societies can reduce violence. Although he concedes that institutional and cultural arguments have some merit, he also insists that his own field theory best explains the different norms and practices that vary across democratic and authoritarian regime types. In his view, democracy is comprised of social fields, constantly in flux and normalizing the bounds of civilized behavior; authoritarianism is static, increasingly rigid, and generating the cleavages over which people resort to violence to secure their survival (or prosperity).

Throughout the text, Rummel meticulously details the various arguments and empirical evidence for democracy's generally pacifying effects. He is never naïve in his portrayal of these effects. He suggests that democracy reduces violence by degrees; that although imperfections persist, democracy remains the most peaceful form of government devised by human societies.

Recent empirical work has generally supported this claim. Indeed, notwith-standing a few definitional quibbles (e.g., Oren, 1995; Rosato, 2003; Ray, 2003), a major war between modern democratic states has still never occurred (Goldstein, 2011). Current studies confirm that civil wars are less likely in democracies (Hegre et al., 2001) and mass killings and democides are virtually unheard of (Davenport, 2007), although critiques abound as to the structural violence imposed by Western democracies on 'periphery' states as well as the ethical and normative implications of democratic peace theory (Galtung, 1990; Hobson, 2011). Terrorism, although somewhat common in democracies, has become something of a substitute for civil war in them (Chenoweth, 2010; Li, 2005), suggesting a decline in severity of political violence in freer states. Such patterns would square well with Rummel's suggestion that democracy reduces most forms of violence, although it would be impossible to eliminate violence from society entirely. His main concern—and the main focus of his book—is on eliminating unrestrained state violence: a goal which he argues is only achievable through the robust construction of democratic societies.

As the book progresses, each chapter addresses common critiques of democratic peace theory on both theoretical and empirical grounds. For example, he was very concerned that the critics of democratic peace were overrating minor skirmishes and equating them to very destructive wars. In responding to the argument by Mansfield & Snyder (1995) that the democratization process can usher in particularly unstable and bloody periods within transitioning states, Rummel argued (p. 102) that Mansfield & Snyder supported this argument by looking at conflict frequency rather than conflict intensity—a crucial conceptual distinction. All conflicts are not equal, according to Rummel. And while transitioning states may be vulnerable to civil conflict, the lethality and global consequence of such internal wars pale in comparison to the far-reaching devastation wrought by major power wars in the twentieth century.

11.3   Nonviolence as the Absence of Unrestrained State Violence

Rummel conceptualized 'nonviolence' in its most elementary way—the lack of violence, and the use of alternatives to war that are not violent. For example, he expects that democracies in disagreement with one another will negotiate, since such forms of conflict resolution are deeply embedded in the culture, social expectations, and practices of democratic societies. He expects democratic leaders to eschew overreaction to domestic political opposition—and to avoid mass killings.

He does not, as far as I can tell, conceive of nonviolence as the active promotion of nonviolent contentious action, or as an active and coercive method of conflict in itself. Around the same time Rummel was completing his thesis, for example, a series of scholars such as Thomas Schelling, Gene Sharp, and Adam Roberts were writing about civilian-based defense—a sort of nonviolent deterrent to foreign occupation where civilians would train in civil disobedience so as to make any foreign occupation too costly and therefore unlikely (see, for instance, Roberts, 1969).

Nor does he conceive of nonviolence in the principled sense in which it is often proffered today (i.e. pacifism), where one would advocate the avoidance of violence simply on the grounds that it is immoral.

Instead, he views nonviolence simply as the absence of violence. As many note, a simple lack of overt violence is a far cry from a positive peace (Galtung, 1996). Rummel is not blind to this—he suggests that a lack of major violence is his goal, and that minor forms of violence will inevitably remain even within democratic states.

Of course, some critics aver that democracy reinforces and promotes structural violence in many different forms (e.g. Hobson, 2011). Rummel sees such critiques as emanating from a leftist bias from within academia, and he sees proponents of such views as influenced by socialists and Marxist critics of classical liberal theory more generally (1997: 100–115). By focusing on the failing of democracies and the structural violence perpetrated by them, he argues, such critics trivialize the scale of violence witnessed by war and democide. That said, he tries to address some of these critiques in his 2007 *Blue Book of Freedom*, in which he claims that political freedom provides economic and food security. However, he seems to miss a primary critique regarding structural violence—that economic, social, and political freedoms are unequally distributed even within 'free' societies based on race, gender, class, or other arbitrary social distinctions. Somewhat surprisingly, Rummel may have missed an opportunity in such dismissals—an opportunity to generate data to demonstrate the value of democracy on various other indicators of social life, such as economic equality, rule of law, quality of life, human development, trust in government, etc. This could have demonstrated that democracies perform well on a number of other indicators besides direct violence. Because his work is so empirically driven, it would make sense to allow empirics to shore up the case for democracy on these other counts as well.

Moreover, one can recognize the benefits of liberal theory without arguing that its applications have been flawless. For instance, the benefits of free societies have been distributed unevenly within them. Rummel himself brings up several examples of direct violence occurring in democracies, such as the beatings of Rodney King (and the subsequent race riots of 1992) in the United States. Such violence occurs quite easily and commonly in democracies. And this is precisely the concern of many critics of democracy and neoliberalism—that they conceal the worst kinds of abuses under the veil of a satisfied, apathetic, and perhaps privileged majority. That is, democracy and justice are not necessarily synonymous with one another, and justice may be a superior indicator of peace compared to democracy.

11.4   The Path to Democracy: Necessarily Bloody?

Rummel expressed frustration at the blunt measures at the disposal of states in bringing about democratic transition. He suggested that many forms of violent intervention, such as the sponsoring of violent rebellions, are anathema to the whole enterprise of both peace and democracy. In *Power Kills*, Rummel (1997: 9) clearly rejected military intervention as a method to bring about democracy in foreign countries. However, he later reversed course on this, suggesting that the invasion of Iraq in 2003 was necessary to stave off Saddam Hussein's brutality and catalyze a wave of democratic transition transitions in the Middle East—and justified in its attempt to form an alliance of democracies to support the invasion (Rummel, 2005a; Tucille, 2014). His prediction was that although an American invasion and occupation would be temporarily painful, it would mostly be ruinous for the dictator and his inner entourage; in the end, the invasion would allow Iraqis the opportunity to liberate themselves from Hussein's tyranny and obtain the power and opportunity to chart their own course forward.

Hence, through one of Rummel's most controversial political stances, he found himself ideologically allied with neoconservative foreign policy elites in endorsing the United States' invasion of Iraq in 2003 (and, indeed, at one point he endorsed censorship on the media on his blog; Rummel, 2005b). Like many neoconservative thinkers, Rummel proved to underestimate the devastating impacts of that war, in terms of both its immediate devastation and its continually bloody aftermath. Some commentators have even suggested that the war in Iraq initiated the period of turmoil in which the Middle East continues to find itself today (Tyler, 2015). It is impossible to know how Rummel would interpret this debacle now—and whether, in hindsight, he would have seen the Iraq War as worth the price in blood and treasure.

In the end, Rummel (1997: 9) suggests that plebiscites or referenda are the ideal ways for people to assert their power and choose their own government. Yet the implementation of this suggestion remains impractical. How are such plebiscites to come about in autocracies? This question is left unanswered. This leaves open the possibility of forced regime change, which has proved ineffective at best and disastrous at worst (Downes & Monten, 2013).

Perhaps he would have revised his views on Iraq if he had known about the realistic alternatives to violent conflict in bringing about democratic transitions. For instance, one wonders what Rummel would have made of the diffusion of mass nonviolent uprisings during the second half of the Twentieth Century—and into the current one (Karatnycky & Ackerman, 2005). Since 1970, the world has witnessed the explosion of mass upheavals characterized primarily by nonviolent forms of contention (Chenoweth & Stephan, 2014). Although states have used exceptional methods to try to counter these uprisings, we have nonetheless seen various waves of these mass movements in Eastern Europe in 1989, the former Soviet Bloc in the mid-2000s, the Arab Spring in 2011, and throughout the industrialized world since 2011. Data on these movements show that mass nonviolent contention has virtually replaced armed uprisings in terms of frequency (Chenoweth & Stephan, 2011). Despite what observers might infer from watching the news, mass violent rebellion is going out of style, and mass nonviolent contention is the new game in town—at least for the time being. As a consequence, nonviolence is now a prominent research agenda within political science (Chenoweth & Cunningham, 2013).

This recent upswing of nonviolent mass movements is not unrelated to Rummel's core interests, and it may even connect to one of his remaining key practical puzzles —that of how countries actually achieve democracy through nonviolent means.

In an article on democratization, Ulfelder (2005) finds that one of the strongest associations is that between mass protests and subsequent democratization.

Similarly, a report by Freedom House finds that 75% of recent democratic transitions were initiated in part (or in whole) by high levels of active civic pressure from below (Karatnycky & Ackerman, 2005). And campaigns of civil resistance—or nonviolence—are more likely to usher in democratic transitions than their violent counterparts (Chenoweth & Stephan, 2011). Indeed, in recent private correspondence, Jay Ulfelder has suggested that he now sees protests as a necessary (but not sufficient) condition in bringing about democratic transitions. According to two separate studies by Johnstad (2010) and Celestino & Gleditsch (2013), such nonviolence-initiated democratic transitions are exceedingly durable.

Rummel's omission of nonviolent resistance from discussion is ironic on several counts. First, his field theory explicitly argues that democratic politics enjoy social fields, which involve '*a high level of nonviolent conflict across the society, the stuff of democratic politics*' (Rummel, 1997: 147, emphasis in original). Indeed, nonviolent conflict—and nonviolent resistance in correcting democratic politics when necessary—is clearly linked to the key mechanisms through which Rummel argues that democracies are more pacific than authoritarian regimes. Rummel clearly knows and understands the literatures on nonviolent conflict, which he cites briefly in a footnote (1997: 102). Yet he totally sidesteps these literatures, seeing nonviolent resistance as an outcome of democracy rather than a cause of it. There is but one mention of Gandhi in the book, but only as a passing reference to charismatic leaders existing within social fields (1997: 156). Nor does Rummel appear to see constructive program (or parallel-institution-building) as a viable way through which societies can pursue models of democracy that suit their own interests. Rummel's volume offers a people-powered explanation for the functioning of elite politics, yet he misses the most potent source of change witnessed in recent history: the people power movements that brought down many of the tyrannical governments he so deplored.

At the same time, Rummel underestimates the plural nature of authoritarian regimes—and the degree to which social fields exist in authoritarian regimes. The past several decades of scholarship on social capital, civil society, and authoritarian regimes, reveals that even in authoritarian regimes, people practice everyday forms of resistance, which can develop into collective outbursts of nonviolent civil disobedience at seemingly a moment's notice (Scott, 1987; Kuran, 1991). Rummel's omission is somewhat ironic, given that he recognizes that democratic governments are not monoliths either (Rummel, 1997: 17). In fact, in many of the authoritarian regimes he cites as having anti-field qualities (USSR, Iran, Chile), people power movements developed and challenged seemingly impenetrable regimes that had, indeed, ruled with excessive brutality (Chenoweth & Stephan, 2011). In other words, social fields may be a cause rather than a consequence of democracy.

11.5 Democracy as the Logical Conclusion?

One wonders what Rummel would think about democracy's current challenges. After the fall of the Soviet Union, many observers averred that humanity had arrived at 'the End of History' (Fukuyama, 1992). Liberal democracy had won the ideological race, and all that remained was to transform the last remaining hold-outs of the authoritarian class age. This optimism about the pacifying effects of democracy became so widely accepted among political elites that it was informing nearly every national security strategy from the early 1990s onward (Miller, 2012). Given the obvious dividends of democracy, it was only a matter of time before all states voluntarily accepted its tenets—or, if not voluntarily, succumbed to these tenets by force. The inevitability of a global system of republics was taken for granted.

However, Freedom House (2015) indicates that 2014 was the 9th year in a row that aggregate democracy scores have declined. With very few exceptions, 2014 was a year of reversal for democracies, with serious backsliding in major global payers like Brazil, Turkey, and Russia, in mid-level states like Hungary, Venezuela, and Azerbaijan, and elsewhere. Given the fact that Rummel saw democracy as inherently superior—and that he viewed the logic of its pacifying effects as universally appealing—one wonders how he might explain these trends.

In fact, the future of democracy, justice, and nonviolence may be linked. Stephan & Burrows (2015) suggest that authoritarian backsliding has been occurring alongside the closure of space for civil society organizations. As authoritarian regimes wise up to the disruptive potential of people power, they try to crush such challenges in their infancy through various forms of smart repression (Chenoweth, 2015). Their attempts to do so are quite revealing about the types of power that truly threaten them.

Although I never met Rudolph Rummel, my guess is that he would have interpreted these trends as deeply troubling because of the constriction of social fields, and that he would predict war and violence as becoming more likely in the midst of such reversals. But because he underestimated the potential of people power movements, his skepticism may have been misplaced. There is a potential solution to the problem of democratization without bloodshed, and the problem of improving unfair and unjust practices within democracies as well: nonviolent resistance.

Indeed, the rise of mass nonviolent movements and their effects on systems of government worldwide may represent one final, unwritten chapter of Rummel's book. He might have concluded that while democracy is a method of nonviolence, it may also be true that 'Nonviolence is the method of achieving democracy.'

References

Celestino, Mauricio Rivera & Kristian Skrede Gleditsch (2013) Fresh carnations or all thorn, no rose? Non-violent campaigns and transitions in autocracies. *Journal of Peace Research* 50(3): 385–400.

Chenoweth, Erica (2010) Democratic competition and terrorist activity. *Journal of Politics* 72(1): 16–30.

Chenoweth, Erica (2015) Trends in civil resistance and authoritarian responses. In: Mathew Burrows & Maria J Stephan (eds) *Is Authoritarianism Staging a Comeback?* Washington, DC: Atlantic Council, 42–50.

Chenoweth, Erica & Kathleen G Cunningham (2013) Understanding nonviolent resistance: An introduction. *Journal of Peace Research* 50(3): 271–276.

Chenoweth, Erica & Maria J Stephan (2011) *Why Civil Resistance Works: The Strategic Logic of Nonviolent Conflict*. New York: Columbia University Press.

Chenoweth, Erica & Maria J Stephan (2014) Drop your weapons: When and why civil resistance works. *Foreign Affairs* 93(4): 94–106.

Davenport, Christian (2007) *State Repression and the Domestic Democratic Peace*. New York: Cambridge University Press.

Downes, Alexander B & Jonathan Monten (2013) Forced to be free? Why foreign-imposed regime change rarely leads to democratization. *International Security* 37(4): 90–131.

Fukuyama, Francis (1992) *The End of History and the Last Man*. New York: Free Press.

Freedom House (2015) *Freedom in the World Annual Report*. Washington, DC: Freedom House.

Galtung, Johan (1990) Cultural violence. *Journal of Peace Research* 27(3): 291–305.

Galtung, Johan (1996) *Peace by Peaceful Means: Peace and Conflict, Development and Civilisation*. London: Sage.

Goldstein, Joshua (2011) *Winning the War on War*. New York: Viking.

Hegre, Håvard; Tanja Ellingsen, Scott Gates, & Nils Petter Gleditsch (2001) Towards a democratic civil peace? Opportunity, grievance, and civil war 1816–1992. *American Political Science Review* 95(1): 33–48.

Hobson, Christopher (2011) Towards a critical theory of democratic peace. *Review of International Studies* 37(4): 1903–1922.

Johnstad, Petter Grahl (2010) Nonviolent democratization: A sensitivity analysis of how transition mode and violence impact the durability of democracy. *Peace and Change* 35(3): 464–482.

Karatnycky, Adrian & Peter Ackerman (2005) *How Freedom is Won: From Civic Resistance to Durable Democracy*. Washington, DC: Freedom House.

Kuran, Timur (1991) Now out of never: The element of surprise in the East European Revolution of 1989. *World Politics* 44(1): 7–48.

Li, Quan (2005) Does democracy promote or reduce transnational terrorist incidents? *Journal of Conflict Resolution* 49(2): 278–297.

Mansfield, Edward & Jack Snyder (1995) Democratization and war. *Foreign Affairs* 74(3): 79–97.

Miller, Paul D (2012) American grand strategy and the democratic peace. *Survival* 54(2): 49–76.

Oren, Ido (1995) The subjectivity of the 'democratic' peace: Changing US perceptions of Imperial Germany. *International Security* 20(2): 147–184.

Ray, James Lee (2003). A Lakatosian view of the democratic peace research program. In: Colin & Miriam Fendius Elman (eds) *Progress in International Relations Theory*. Cambridge: MIT Press, 205–243.

Rosato, Sebastian (2003) The flawed logic of democratic peace theory. *American Political Science Review* 97(4): 585–602.

Roberts, Adam (ed.) (1969) *Civilian Resistance as a National Defence: Non-violent Action against Aggression*. New York: Penguin.

Rummel, RJ (1997) *Power Kills: Democracy as a Method of Nonviolence*. New Brunswick: Transaction.

Rummel, RJ (2005a) R. J. Rummel: Scowcroft just doesn't get it. *Free Republic Online* (October 24), available at http://www.freerepublic.com/focus/bloggers/1510848/posts, accessed 13 September 2015.

Rummel, RJ (2005b) Censor the media. FreedomsPeaceBlog, available at http://web.archive.org/web/20050807073933/http://freedomspeace.blogspot.com/2005/02/censor-media.html, accessed 13 September 2015.

Rummel, RJ (2007) *The Blue Book of Freedom*. New York: Cumberland House Publishing.

Scott, James (1987) *Weapons of the Weak: Everyday Forms of Peasant Resistance*. New Haven, CT: Yale University Press.

Stephan, Maria J & Mat Burrows (eds) (2015) *Is Authoritarianism Staging a Comeback?* Washington, DC: Atlantic Council.

Tucille, Jerome D (2014) A moment for the late Rudolph Rummel, who documented the murderous nature of government. *Reason Magazine Online*, at: http://reason.com/blog/2014/05/12/a-moment-for-the-late-rj-rummel-who-docu, accessed 12 September 2015.

Tyler, Taylor (2015) Iraq turmoil directly caused by US invasion, says former UN Secretary General. *HNGN News Online,* at: http://www.hngn.com/articles/89278/20150502/former-un-secretary-general-current-turmoil-in-iraq-directly-caused-by-u-s-invasion.htm, accessed 12 September 2015.

Ulfelder, Jay (2005) Contentious collective action and the breakdown of authoritarian regimes. *International Political Science Review* 26(3): 311–334.

Chapter 12
The Comparative Analysis of Mass Atrocities and Genocide

Barbara Harff

Rudolph Rummel and I are both products of Northwestern University's Ph.D. program—although I graduated 18 years later.[1] Thanks to him, I already knew something about factor analysis, having read his dissertation. I was equally familiar with arguments about peace among democratic states, because my major was in international relations with a minor in jurisprudence (i.e. international law) and another in comparative studies. The democratic peace argument filtered much later into comparative studies of civil conflict in democratic societies and made much sense to me in theory, the way it became a major focus in Rudy's work on mass death and genocide.

My task here is to assess Rummel's contribution to genocide studies, which has been the focus of my own scholarly career. Twenty years ago, I reviewed *Death by Governments* critically (Harff, 1996: 117–119) and I will use this book to answer some of the criticism he had to deal with after it was published in 1994. Of course, his work was also hailed at the time as a major contribution because it documented how many people were killed by authoritarian and communist governments in the 20th century. My focus will be first on his definition of democide in comparison with the narrower definition of genocide, second on data issues, and third on some implications of his theoretical focus, mainly his democratic peace argument.

Barbara Harff, b. 1942, is Professor of Political Science Emerita at the US Naval Academy and has been Distinguished Visiting Professor at Clark University's Strassler Center for Holocaust and Genocide Studies. She helped plan the 2004 Stockholm International Forum on the Prevention of Genocide and co-founded with Yehuda Bauer the Genocide Prevention Advisory Network (GPANet.org). Her books include *Genocide and Human Rights: International Legal and Political Issues* (1984) and, with Ted Robert Gurr, *Ethnic Conflict in World Politics* (1994, revised ed. 2003); Email: barbaraharff@aol.com.

[1]This chapter is based on a contribution to a panel at the 56th Annual Convention of the International Studies Association, New Orleans, LA, 18–21 February 2015.

© The Author(s) 2017
N.P. Gleditsch (ed.), *R.J. Rummel: An Assessment of His Many Contributions*,
SpringerBriefs on Pioneers in Science and Practice 37,
DOI 10.1007/978-3-319-54463-2_12

12.1   Definitional Issues

Rudy devoted five books to the systematic analysis of democide, four of them published within a span of five years. *Lethal Politics* (1990) documented Soviet mass killings after 1917, *China's Bloody Century* (1991) was the second, and the third covered *Nazi Genocide and Mass Murder* (1992). The capstone was *Death by Government* (1994), which summarized the empirical and theoretical basis of his concept of democide, with documentation of many other cases. The fifth book, *Statistics of Democide* (1998) showed just how thoroughly and carefully he compiled and analyzed the data he used.

Definitions are crucial to a new and broad concept like democide. Rummel (1994: 42) summarizes a chapter-long discussion with this: 'A death constitutes democide if it is the intentional killing of an unarmed or disarmed person by government agents acting in their authoritative capacity and pursuant to government policy or high command'. He adds that it encompasses reckless and wanton disregard for the lives of forced labor and concentration camp victims; 'unofficial' killings by private groups; extrajudicial summary killings; and mass deaths that occurred because governments ignored or perpetrated their causes, as in deliberate famines. Elsewhere (p. 37) he adds that it includes killings by de facto governments, i.e. rebels or warlords. One major category of intentional killing not counted as democide consists of the military casualties of international war. His data show that civilian deaths by government in the 20th century outnumber military deaths by a ratio of about 6 to 1 (pp. 15, 20).

In my review, I pointed out that 'clear conceptualization is a prerequisite to sound explanation' (Harff, 1996: 118). Rudy's definition of democide meets this criterion. Moreover it has both a theoretical and normative basis: he uses it to guide his cumulation of data on mass killings by totalitarian and autocratic government, which he systematically contrasts with the much lower incidence of mass killings by democratic governments. So how does this compare with the concept of genocide and its theoretical uses? Rummel points out that democide comprises genocides, but not all genocidal phenomena as detailed by Raphael Lemkin and codified in the UN's 1948 Genocide Convention.[2] The Convention includes policies whose intent is to cause mental harm, to inflict conditions of life aimed to bring about the group's physical destruction in whole or part, and measures intended to prevent birth. Specifically, the crime of genocide is the intent to eliminate 'in whole or part' a national, racial, ethnic, or religious group. Insofar as this entails direct killing of group members, it is included in democide. The data collections created to operationalize this definition (for example by Harff, 2003 and Fein, 1993) focus on killings, not on mental or cultural harm. Moreover, the working definitions of empiricists almost invariably include politicide, the killing of people because of their political and social affiliations. Indeed, Lemkin included destruction of a people's

---

[2]UN General Assembly, *Convention on the Prevention and Punishment of the Crime of Genocide*, General Assembly Resolution 26, 8 December 1948.

political and social institutions, but the politics of the UN General Assembly precluded inclusion of this type of mass killing, now generally called politicide.

There is an obvious normative purpose to the Genocide Convention and the empirical research carried out in its name: to clarify the causes and manifestations of genocide (and politicide) so that preventive actions are justified, and required, by international law. In short, conceptually democide includes all the mass killings associated with genocide and politicide, but also many others that are not aimed at the intentional destruction of a particular group. And normatively their objectives also are somewhat different. The study of democide leads to condemnation of entire categories of governments because they are at risk of killing large numbers of citizens; comparative study of genocide aims to help identify specific governments for specific crimes against humanity.

12.2   Data Questions

Compiling global data is hazardous and will inevitably invite chagrin and criticism from country experts. Case study people have a problem with systematic data because they often think they know better what happened in one particular country. I have sympathized with this view, because my area expertise was the Middle East. But when empiricists focus on global data, we have to consider 190 countries and must rely on country experts selectively. When we look for patterns and test explanations, we cannot expect absolute precision, in fact we do not require it.

In my critical review I said that 'from an empirical viewpoint, there are problems with Rummel's data', that is, 'he chooses numbers of death that almost always are skewed in the direction of the highest guesses' (Harff, 1996: 118). The most damaging critique came from an anonymous blogger, who argued that Rummel had no business writing a book on a subject matter that he did not master. Five books seem to me sufficient evidence of mastery, if not necessarily total accuracy. That is in fact an inevitable problem for those seeking reliable data on mass casualties. Few perpetrators make accurate counts of their victims. Estimates diverge widely, and Rummel is careful to gather and report multiple estimates for any given event. Thus, his detailed writings refer to ranges of estimates, but rather than repeat them at every turn he usually uses average or median numbers. Then he adds them for total effect: '169,198,000 Murdered' (the title of Chap. 1) globally from 1900 to 1986. Later he enlarged this to 262 million, after increasing the figure for colonial democide and concluding that the deaths due to the Chinese famine of the Great Leap Forward in 1959–61 were an intentional consequence of government policy.[3]

Another reason for being critical about the democide data was that Rummel could have provided more useful datasets by focusing specifically on more precisely defined concepts such as geno/politicide, mass atrocities, ethnic wars, or state

---

[3]See at: http://www.hawaii.edu/powerkills/20TH.HTM.

terrorism. All of these specific types of state-implicated violence have been the subject of comparative empirical studies aimed at identifying their causes. The concept of democide is so wide that it is inevitable that Rudy's numbers of death are higher than those for genocide specifically.

A third critique comes from case study scholars who may argue that one should pay attention to additional episodes that did not make a particular list, or that numbers of people dead were higher, lower or altogether too badly documented to warrant any reasonable estimates. As someone who had tried to identify all cases of geno/politicide since World War II,[4] I fully understand what it takes to collect reliable, unimpeachable global data. It is impossible. The best we can do is to seek advice about additional episodes, and to report ranges of fatality estimates, as Rummel does.

Over time I have become more critical of country experts who challenge systematic empirical studies. Case studies are scarce, of dubious accuracy, or non-existent for some episodes of mass death, and estimates vary greatly. Some episodes dating back to before say, 1918 happened in countries that no longer exist or in countries that did not yet exist. Colonial authorities in Africa and Asia kept scarce or no records of birth or death rates. Perpetrators seldom keep records of their misdeeds and if they do, as in Nazi Germany, death estimates often are greatly underestimated or attributed to circumstances rather than deliberate policies.

To make the point clearer, let us take a closer look at two 20th century episodes of genocide. Who among scholars is correct in estimating the numbers who died during the Holocaust? If we treat the Shoah as genocide, we count as its victims about 5.5 million people—Jews, Roma, and others—who were killed because of their ethnic, racial, religious, or national group affiliation. What happened to the others who died, because of their political affiliations, or were systematically starved (see especially Russian prisoners of war) or were victims of what today we would call crimes against humanity during war, i.e. atrocities? Should we ignore the deaths of millions because of some arbitrary definition? The concept of democide avoids this essential problem. By Rummel's estimates 20,946,000 died at the hands of Nazi Germany from 1933 to 1945, of whom 16,315,000 were victims of genocide (Rummel, 1994: 4).

For another more recent example, consider Cambodia (1975–79). Some scholars argued that under the Genocide Convention it was not a genocide, because the victims belonged to the same ethnic group as the perpetrators. Senseless as it may seem today, it became an issue because of the primary focus on the group identity of victims. This led these scholars to think that victims had to be the 'OTHER,' some identifiable group apart from the perpetrators, although the language of the convention never says that genocide cannot be committed by people who are ethnic, racial, national, or religious kin of the victims. If we follow that logic, Germans killing Germans during World War II or Khmers killing Khmers in Cambodia cannot be counted as victims of genocide. In the case of Cambodia, the concept of

---

[4]Harff & Gurr (1988) and many revisions through Harff (2003).

'auto-genocide' became part of some scholars' definitional arsenal. The concept of democide avoids this conceptual trap.

Any internal conflict situation carries the seeds of genocide. We know that typically victims have multiple identities, thus gender, culture, economic and social status, and political affiliation may play a secondary or close to a primary role in their victimization. Genocidal patterns often are readily apparent. In the search for motives and intent we should analyze killing patterns. Thus in the case of Cambodia intent is not hard to discover. What seemed irrational to outside observers such as killing loyal cadres, makes sense when one took a close look at the confused ideology of the Khmer Rouge. This was an ideology reminiscent of Jacobinism, a revolution that devoured itself. Many victims were simply not wanted by the regime for diverse reasons that changed over time.

I chose to call this genocidal episode a politicide, having coined the concept to account for victims who were killed primarily because of their political or social affiliations. I used estimates from various sources that ranged from 1.9 million to 3 million people killed in four years of Khmer Rouge rule of a population of about 7 million.

Later, I came across a demographic study conducted by the CIA suggesting a likely death toll of 1.2–1.3 million dead and I lowered my estimates. In general, I think it is necessary at first look to assume higher death rates, because the perpetrators are unlikely to tell and demographic data in poor third-world countries are of questionable accuracy. When I looked at Rudy's sources for Cambodia I recognized all (for example Chandler, 1991, and Kiernan & Boua, 1982). I became cautious about trusting these sources, especially when I realized that there was an ideological bent to these scholars who, at least during their early careers, seemed to be apologists for the Khmer Rouge regime. Rummel, in his analysis of Cambodia, categorizes deaths from 1967 to 1987 as caused by war and rebellion (514,000), famine and disease (280,000) and democide (3,186,000). Given that he includes all victims of government killings, his estimates are consistent with those of others.

Nowhere in *Death by Government* is it more obvious what drives Rummel to collect data than in the case of Cambodia. He describes the indescribable with great passion and revulsion. I share his sorrow and anger about the cruelty and sheer inhumanity that led to the deaths of the old, the feeble, babies, pregnant women, and so many others. Cambodia at large was a Nazi type concentration camp for all but a few—the Hell State as Rummel calls it. In 1981, I was in Thailand to interview survivors of the Cambodian genocide in a makeshift refugee camp. The detailed descriptions of unspeakable horrors have never left me. I relived it when Rummel described the slaughter of a pregnant woman whose fetus was hanged to wither. For years it haunted me to think that a human being could act as a wild beast and that observers, near or distant, did nothing. As we know all too well, helpers in the real world are a rare breed in the face of danger to their own survival, but then few of us have ever been in such situations. Rummel was enraged by what he heard and saw. This is what drove him to report how, how many, why, and when the victims died. This is the kinship I feel, each death that we report prompts us to mourn a life lost.

12.3 Discovering Intent

Democide according to Rudy, as noted above, 'is the murder of any person or people by a government, including genocide, politicide, and mass murder.' Given his definition, he has to deal with all the issues above and add victims killed during other forms of conflict, such as civil wars and pogroms, in which peoples are murdered by states for any reason, as in Syria today, or during World War II, as were Polish civilians and officers. Rummel adds that the killing has to be intentional not indiscriminate, thus, he is very much in the same position as any genocide scholar seeking to discover intent.

To reiterate, when we count victims of genocide we need to look for groups that have a common identity as described in the Genocide Convention. We also recognize that perpetrators may attribute a collective identity to them of which they may not be conscious—as 'enemies of the state' or 'old people' who stand in the way of social change. By contrast, Rummel includes in democide both geno/politicide and mass murder, all instances in which governments kill or cause the death of peoples because of their religion, race, language, ethnicity, national origin, class, politics, speech, actions construed as opposing the government or wrecking social policy, or by virtue of their relationship to such people (Rummel, 1994: 36–37). These categories of peoples go way beyond the official definition of genocide by the inclusion of class, politics, speech, and kinship. The latter categories could be construed as part of what I call politicide, but kinship is not part of the definition either in the Genocide Convention or in the discussion of political groups. By his definition, victims of massacres include the killings of prisoners of war and captured rebels, an extension that probably is acceptable to most scholars dealing with mass violence.

Intent is a necessary condition for identifying genocide and politicide. Rummel deals with it by arguing that democide includes the targeting of noncombatants during a war or violent conflict out of hatred or revenge, or to depopulate an enemy region, or to terrorize civilians into surrender; also included is torture leading to death. Essentially he includes all intentional killings, but excludes 'actions taken against armed civilians during mob actions, executions for capital crimes and death of noncombatants during attacks where the primary targets are military.' How to discover intent in democide is less complicated than in geno/politicide. In geno/politicide group members are targeted whereas in democide they can be either members of groups or individuals. Thus, in democide it is not a question whether group survival is at stake, i.e. how many people need to be killed to destroy the group in part or whole, because he counts anybody systematically killed by a government.

In the early days of genocide studies we had difficulties with how best to discover intent. I argued that we can be confident that the killings are intentional when we see that a particular group's members are targeted repeatedly and in a sustained campaign. Rummel sees as intentional all killings that are premeditated and carried out by governments or their agents, even if the killings happen through malign neglect, such as mass starvation, or through indiscriminate bombings of settlements, as in Syria now. For him, intent is discovered through looking at outcomes. Any action by a government or their agents that leads inevitably to death is likely a case of democide. Today, genocide scholars have less disagreement about discovering intent. Act and outcome matter most. If ISIL members massacre Alawites or Yazidis repeatedly, it is a genocide; here we come close to Rummel's perspective of what matters most.

The perpetrators of genocide and democide include both governments and de facto governments. When I first read of de facto governments I was intrigued by the way Rudy included competing governments, that is rebel organizations that control part of a country. For me, the category government was also too narrow, because in some cases genocide was committed by non-governmental groups acting with an implicit government sanction, as in Sudan and the eastern Congo. I called de facto governments contending authorities, although this leads to real problems with statistical analyses that focus on states as the primary actors.

In one other respect, though, the significance of fatality estimates varies between genocide studies and democide. Genocide by definition is not dependent on numbers of people killed. The destruction of a group is at stake when the leadership is annihilated, which takes the life out of the group. Hypothetically, victims could number in the few hundreds. A case in point is the persecution of Ba'hais by the revolutionary Iranian regime, with a few thousands killed; or Syria where some 30,000 members of the Muslims Brotherhood and other civilians were murdered by the Hafez Assad regime in 1981/82. We need to be able to identify victim groups, and should be able to identify the proportions of people eliminated. But even the death of 30,000 Muslim Brothers is scarcely a blip in the data on democide.

12.4 Theoretical Issues

Let me now return to the democratic peace argument. Rudy, like many other scholars, contended that democracies are unlikely to fight each other. Among democracies, diplomacy replaces bullets. Domestically, the ballot box has the same moderating effects. He argues that if we check power through democratic freedoms we would not have democide (Rummel, 1994: 27). Quoting Lord Acton, Rummel (1994: 19) concludes that 'power kills, and absolute power kills absolutely'. This is a categorical statement about a relationship that is in fact probabilistic. A larger theoretical question it raises is why do some totalitarian and authoritarian regimes commit megamurders while others do not? Saudi Arabia, for example, is one of the most authoritarian states in the contemporary world, yet state executions only number in the hundreds. Uzbekistan is a similar example. And on the democratic side, Sri Lanka is one clear case of a democratic regime that in 1989–90 authorized military squads to track down and summarily execute members and suspected supporters of the JVP (Peoples Liberation Party), which had begun its second rebellion that threatened to overthrow the state. Between 13,000 and 30,000 were killed in this politicide—not a megamurder, of course, but a challenge to Rudy's basic argument.

A regime's power is a permissive condition, not a root cause of mass violence. Empirical research on causes of genocides and on civil wars has provided much evidence on the preconditions of mass murder. Krain (1997, 2000) shows that genocides and politicides often occur in the immediate aftermath of abrupt power transitions, when new leaders suppress their opposition. Valentino, Huth & Balch-Lindsay (2004) show that 'excess casualties' (including genocidal-like mass atrocities) are most likely to occur in civil wars in which regimes face major armed challenges—an explanation that fits the Sri Lanka example. My research on the preconditions of genocide shows that regimes based on ethnic minorities are particularly likely to use genocidal strategies against majority ethnicities—as in contemporary Syria. My results also show that regimes with exclusionary ideologies often resort to mass killings of opponents (Harff, 2003). Examination of Rudy's list of megamurders shows that the greatest death tolls—notably in Soviet Russia, PRC China, Nazi Germany, and Cambodia—were the result of deadly social engineering aimed at implementing an ideological imperative. But where does this leave us? His data on democide are descriptions in search of multivariate explanation.

In my 1996 review, I characterized Rudy's argument about power and democracy as a categorical imperative and a case of wishful thinking. The implication for international policy is that the best (only?) defense against democide is to encourage democratic transitions. But, then 'not all authoritarian or traditional polities are likely to commit genocide, nor are the local traditions and political cultures of many third-world states necessarily compatible with democratic traditions' (Harff, 1996: 119). We also know that failed efforts to democratize countries have contributed directly to episodes of mass murder and genocide, as in Rwanda and Burundi. My 2003 article reports a test of a structural model of the antecedents of geno/politicide, in which political system characteristics was one of six significant variables. Autocracy and democracy were indexed using the Polity dataset. I found state failure in states with autocratic regimes to be three and a half times more likely to lead to geno/politicides than failure in democratic regimes if they occur in the context of other risk factors identified (Harff, 2003: 66). Rummel was partially correct, but it needed a more careful analysis to evaluate the claim that democracy is a sovereign remedy for democide. He could have tested his claim, recognizing that democracy is a matter of degree, using the Polity data with which he was familiar. But in none of his work, as far as I know, does he report empirical tests of his basic thesis. And perhaps that was unnecessary because the enormity of his democide data collection points unambiguously to the guilt of totalitarian and (some) authoritarian states.

What are we to remember about Rummel? He was a scholar who did a monumental job in collecting data and information, one of the very few scholars of mass murder who was systematic and global in his quest to document genocides, politicides and mass murder, and to identify a root cause. A passionate man, bold and courageous in stating his ideas. He held that liberalism, unabridged political participation, freedom of the press, and an independent judiciary were the best guarantees to protect individuals from those who preach that the ideal society can only be achieved through murder, repression, and enslavement. If he were to chronicle the contemporary rise of ISIL or Syria's descent into politicide, he would have thought that humanity had heard nothing.

References

Chandler, David P (1991) *The Tragedy of Cambodian History.* New Haven, CT: Yale University Press.

Fein, Helen (1993) Accounting for genocide after 1945: Theories and some findings. *International Journal on Minority and Group Rights* 1(2): 79–106.

Harff, Barbara (1996) Review of RJ Rummel: Death by Government. *Journal of Interdisciplinary History* 27(1): 117–119.

Harff, Barbara (2003) No lessons learned from the Holocaust? Assessing risks of genocide and political mass murder since 1955. *American Political Science Review* 97(1): 75–90.

Harff, Barbara & Ted Robert Gurr (1988) Toward empirical theory of genocides and politicides: Identification and measurement of cases since 1945. *International Studies Quarterly* 32(3): 359–371.

Kiernan, Ben & Chanthou Boua (1982) *Peasants and Politics in Kampuchea 1942–1981.* London: Zed.

Krain, Matthew (1997) State-sponsored mass murder: The onset and severity of genocides and politicides. *Journal of Conflict Resolution* 41(3): 331–360.

Krain, Matthew (2000) Democracy, internal war, and state sponsored mass murder. *Human Rights Review* 1(3): 40–48.

Rummel, Rudolph J (1990) *Lethal Politics: Soviet Genocide and Mass Murder since 1917.* New Brunswick, NJ: Transaction.

Rummel, Rudolph J (1991) *China's Bloody Century: Genocide and Mass Murder since 1900.* New Brunswick, NJ: Transaction.

Rummel, Rudolph J (1992) *Democide: Nazi Genocide and Mass Murder.* New Brunswick, NJ: Transaction.

Rummel, Rudolph J (1994) *Death by Government.* New Brunswick, NJ: Transaction.

Rummel, Rudolph J (1998) *Statistics of Democide: Genocide and Mass Murder since 1900.* Muenster: LIT.

Ulfelder, Jay & Benjamin Valentino (2008) Assessing risks of state-sponsored mass killing. *Social Science Research Network*, http://papers.ssrn.com/sol3/papers.cfm?abstract_id=1703426.

Valentino, Benjamin; Paul Huth & Dylan Balch-Lindsay (2004) 'Draining the sea': Mass killing and guerrilla warfare. *International Organization* 58(2): 375–407.

Chapter 13
Curriculum Vitae and Publications

Rudolph J. Rummel

13.1 Curriculum Vitae

Born 21 October 21 1932, Cleveland, OH
Died 2 March 2014, Kaneohe, HI

Family
Wife: Grace S (deceased 2013), daughters: Dawn A and Lei S

Education
BA, political science, 1959, University of Hawaii
MA, political science, 1961, University of Hawaii
BA equivalent credits, mathematics, 1961, University of Hawaii
Ph.D., political science, 1963, Northwestern University

Honors, Fellowships, and Grants

Phi Beta Kappa; Phi Kappa Phi; Omicron Delta Kappa
Carl F Knoblock Prize in Government for Scholastic Achievement, 1959
George Washington Honor Medal Award, Freedom Foundation at Valley Forge, 1977
Guest, International Cultural Society of Korea, August 1986
Selection of *Applied Factor Analysis* as a 'Citation Classic' by Institute for Scientific
    Information, 1987
Nominated for the United States Peace Institute Peace Medal
Congressional Reception on *Death by Government*, Washington, DC, November 1994
Graduate Convocation Speaker, University of Hawaii, May 1995
Panel in honor of Rummel's research, Annual Convention of the International Studies
    Association, Chicago, IL, 1995
Nobel Peace Prize frequent nominee beginning in 1996
Third Place, 1997 Grawemeyer Award for Ideas Improving World Order
Susan Strange Award of the International Studies Association for having intellectually
    most challenged the field, 1999

© The Author(s) 2017
N.P. Gleditsch (ed.), *R.J. Rummel: An Assessment of His Many Contributions*,
SpringerBriefs on Pioneers in Science and Practice 37,
DOI 10.1007/978-3-319-54463-2_13

Lifetime Achievement Award from the Conflict Processes Section, American Political
  Science Association, 2003
International Association of Genocide Scholars Award for Distinguished Lifetime
  Contribution to the Field of Genocide and Democide Studies and Prevention, 2005

Fellowships and Scholarships

Institute of World Affairs Scholarship, 1959
Northwestern University International Relations Program Fellowship, 1961, 1962

Grants

National Science Foundation grants, 1963–64, 1964–66, 1966, 1966–68, 1972–74
Advanced Research Projects Agency (Department of Defense) grants, 1967–69, 1969–
  70, 1970–71, 1971–72, 1972–73, 1974–75
Ilhae Institute, 1986–87
United States Institute of Peace, 1988–90, 1990–92

Professional Positions

Director, NSF Dimensionality of Nations Project, 1962–63
Principal Investigator and Director, Dimensionality of Nations Project, 1963–75
Assistant Professor of Political Science, Indiana University, 1963–64
Assistant Professor of Political Science, Yale University, 1964–66
Visiting Assistant Professor, University of Hawaii, 1966–67
Research Political Scientist, Social Science Research Institute, University of Hawaii,
  1966–68
Associate Professor, University of Hawaii, 1967–68
Director, the PATH Institute of Research on International Problems, 1974–77
Vice President, Political Economic Risk Consultants, 1976–78
Professor of Political Science, University of Hawaii, 1968–95
President, Haiku Institute of Peace Research, 1987–95
Professor Emeritus, University of Hawaii, 1996–2014

Professional Activities

Consultant

Laboratory for Electronics, 1962
Bendix Aerospace Systems Division, 1965–72
Special Operations Research Office, Department of Army, 1965–66
JCS/ARPA Simulated International Processes Project, Northwestern University, 1965–
  67
Political Science Research Library, Yale University, 1964–66
Yale Political Data Program, 1964–66
National Science Foundation, 1965, 1966, 1974, 1979, 1982, 1983
Advanced Research Projects Agency, 1965–66
General Electric, TEMPO, 1969–70
Global Political Research, 1976
Stanford Research Center, Washington, DC, 1976–81
Planning Research Corporation, Washington, DC, 1978–83
CACI, Washington, DC, 1982

Editorships

Associate Editor, *Journal of Conflict Resolution*, 1968–71
Interim Editor, *Interpolimetrics Newsletter*, 1970–72

Editorial Boards

Strategic Review, 1977–82
Orbis, 1981–84
International Journal on World Peace, 1984–2014
Westview Press Studies in International Security, 1987–90

Chairmanships

Institute for Defense Analysis/Advanced Research Projects Agency Conference on Basic Political Science Research, 1967
Quantitative International Politics Society, 1969–70
University of Hawaii Faculty-Student Council, 1970
Interpolimetrics Society 1971–72

Board and Committee Memberships

International Relations Archive Advisory Committee, 1968–70
Constitutional Revision Committee, American Political Science Association, 1970–71
Board of Research Consultants, Institute for Foreign Policy Analysis, 1978–86
Republican National Committee, Advisory Council on National Security and International Relations, 1977–80
Negotiation Institute (New York), 1979–86

Founder

Interpolimetrics Society, 1972
PATH Institute of Research on International Problems, 1974
Political Economic Risk Consultants, 1976
Haiku Institute of Peace Research, 1987

Presentations (Excluding Speeches)

Peace Research Conference, University of Chicago, 1964
Peace Research Conference, University of Pennsylvania, 1965
Project CAMELOT Conference, Airlie House, Warrenton, VA, 1965
Computers and the Policy Making Community Institute, Lawrence Radiation Laboratory, Berkeley, CA, 1966
ARPA Behavioral Science Symposium on Political Science Research, Arlington, VA, 1967
Second ARPA Behavioral Science Symposium on Political Science Research, Institute for Defense Analysis, Arlington, VA, 1967
International Politics Theory Symposium, Center for Advanced Study in the Behavioral Sciences, Stanford, CA, 1968
Long Range Planning and Forecasting Conference, Holloman Air Force Base, NM, 1969
Peace Research Conference, Rome, Italy, 1969
Peace Research Conference, London School of Economics, London, England, 1969

First Asian Peace Research Conference, Tokyo, Japan, 1969

Quantitative Political Science Meeting, Monterey, CA, 1970

Annual Convention of the International Studies Association, 1970, 1972, 1974, 1977, 1995

ARPA Utilization Conference, Airlie House, Warrenton, VA, 1972

NSF Conference on the Successes and Failures of International Relations Research, Ojai, CA, 1973

Communication and Peace in the Pacific, East-West Center, Honolulu, HI, 1973

International Transactions for the Future Conference, East-West Center, Honolulu, HI, 1975

NSF Conference on Control Theory in International Relations Research, Indiana University, Bloomington, IN, 1975

Peace and Unification on the Korean Peninsula in a New International Order, Seoul, Korea, 1975

American Security Council, Washington, DC, 1976

Alfred P Sloan School of Management, MIT, Boston, MA, 1977

Symposium on Nuclear Strength—A Faustian Bargain?, University of Idaho, Moscow, ID, 1977

Workshop on Appraisal of Technology Assessment, University of Dayton Research Institute, Dayton, OH, 1977

International Symposium in Search of a Peace System in Northeast Asia, Tokyo, Japan, 1978

Conference on Prospect for World Peace, Florida Atlantic University, Boca Raton, FL, 1979

US Commission on Proposals for the National Academy of Peace and Conflict Resolution, Honolulu, HI, 1980

Humanities Conference, Honolulu, HI, 1980

Colloquium on Defending a Free Society, University of Dayton, Dayton, OH, 1981

Foreign Policy Research Institute, Philadelphia, PA, 1981

Defense Intelligence Agency, Department of Defense, Washington, DC, 1981

Asian Studies Center, American University, Washington, DC, 1981

Seminar, National Defense University, Washington, DC, 1981

Reason Foundation Conference on Defending a Free Society, Santa Barbara, CA, 1983

Professor's World Peace Academy Conference on the Sino-Soviet-American Triad, Los Angeles, CA, 1985

Sogang Institute for East Asian Studies and Korean Association for International Relations, Seoul, Korea, 1986

International Conference on The Strategic Defense Initiative: Implications for the Asian Community, Seoul, Korea, 1986

United States Institute of Peace Conference, Airlie House, Airlie, VA, 1988

Center for International Affairs, Harvard University, 1989

United States Institute of Peace Conference, Washington, DC, 1990

American Bar Association Meeting on 'The Rule of Law in US Foreign Policy and the New World Order', Washington, DC, 1991

Program on Nonviolent Sanctions in Conflict and Defense, Center for International Affairs, Harvard University, 1992

Department of Political Science, Florida Atlantic University, Tallahasee, FL, 1992

Center for National Security Law and American Bar Association Conference on
    Democracy and the Rule of Law in Foreign Policy, Washington, DC, 1993
Department of Political Science, Florida Atlantic University, Tallahasee, FL, 1994
Center for International Affairs, Harvard University, 1994
School of Law, University of Virginia, 1994
Center for National Security Law, University of Virginia, 1994
Congressional Reception on *Death by Government,* Washington, DC, 1994
Seminar by Academics of the Second Amendment, Miami, FL, 1994
Center on Law, Ethics and National Security Conference, Durham, NC, 1995
School of Law, University of Virginia, 1995
Convocation Speech, University of Hawaii, 1996

13.2 Publications, Reports, and Papers

13.2.1 Books

Applied Factor Analysis. Evanston, IL: Northwestern University Press, 1970.
Dimensions of Nations. Beverly Hills, CA: Sage, 1976.
Peace Endangered: The Reality of Détente. Beverly Hills, CA: Sage, 1976.
Field Theory Evolving. Beverly Hills, CA: Sage, 1977.
Dynamics of Power: The US-USSR Arms Field. Honolulu, HI: Department of Political
    Science, University of Hawaii, 1977.
Understanding Correlation. Honolulu, HI: Department of Political Science, University
    of Hawaii, 1978.
National Attributes and Behavior: Dimensions, Linkages and Groups, 1950–65.
    Beverly Hills, CA: Sage, 1979.
Understanding Conflict and War. Vols. 1–5. Beverly Hills, CA: Sage, 1975–81.
Vol. 1: *The Dynamic Psychological Field,* 1975
Vol. 2: *The Conflict Helix,* 1976
Vol. 3: *Conflict in Perspective,* 1977
Vol. 4: *War, Power, Peace,* 1979
Vol. 5: *The Just Peace,* 1981
Analyzing Population Policy and Demographic Change. Calcutta: Prajna, 1981.
In The Minds of Men: Principles Toward Understanding and Waging Peace. Seoul:
    Sogang University Press, 1984.
*Freedom or Violence: On the Inverse Relationship between Political Freedom and
    Collective Violence.* Honolulu, HI: Department of Political Science, University of
    Hawaii, 1986.
Lethal Politics: Soviet Genocides and Mass Murders 1917–87. Rutgers, NJ:
    Transaction, 1990.
*The Conflict Helix: Principles and Practices of Interpersonal, Social, and International
    Conflict and Cooperation.* Rutgers, NJ: Transaction, 1991.
China's Bloody Century: Genocide and Mass Murder since 1900. Rutgers, NJ:
    Transaction, 1991.
Democide: Nazi Genocide and Mass Murder. Rutgers, NJ: Transaction, 1992.

Death by Government: Genocide and Mass Murder in the Twentieth Century. NJ: Transaction, 1994.

The Miracle that Is Freedom. Martin Institute, University of Idaho, 1996.

Statistics of Democide. Center on National Security and Law, University of Virginia, 1997. Münster: LIT, 1998.

Power Kills. NJ: Transaction, 1997.

Saving Lives, Enriching Life: Freedom as a Right, and a Moral Good, 2001, http://www.hawaii.edu/powerkills/WFA.BOOKSAVING.PDF.

Lo Stato, Il Democidio, La Guerra: Antologia Di Seritti Sulla Violenza Dei Governi. Treviglio: Presso Tipografia Eliografia Saccardo, 2002.

Rummel's Libertarian Peace Theory. [Collected Works in Korean]. Edited by Rhee Sang-Woo, 2002.

The Blue Book of Freedom. Nashville, TN: Cumberland House, 2007.

Freedom's Principles, 2008, https://www.hawaii.edu/powerkills/FP.PDF.

Never Again novels, published by Llumina Press (Fort Lauderdale, FL). They can be freely downloaded in .pdf format from https://www.hawaii.edu/powerkills/NH.HTM.

War & Democide Never Again, 2004

Nuclear Holocaust Never Again, 2004

Reset Never Again, 2004

Red Terror Never Again, 2005

Genocide Never Again, 2005

Never Again? 2005

Never Again: Ending War, Democide, & Famine through Democratic Freedom. Nonfiction supplement, 2005, https://www.hawaii.edu/powerkills/NA.SUPPLE-MENT.PDF.

13.2.2   Articles and Chapters

Dimensions of conflict behavior within and between nations. *General Systems: Yearbook of the Society for General Systems* 8, 1963: 1–50.

Testing some possible predictors of conflict behavior within and between nations. *Peace Research Society, Papers* 1, Chicago Conference, 1963: 79–111.

A field theory of social action with application to conflict within nations. *General Systems: Yearbook of the Society for General Systems* 10, 1965: 183–211.

A social field theory of foreign conflict behavior. *Peace Research Society Papers* 4, Cracow Conference, 1966: 131–150.

The Dimensionality of Nations Project. In: *Comparing Nations. The Use of Quantitative Data in Cross-National Research.* Edited by Richard Merritt & Stein Rokkan. New Haven, CT: Yale University Press, 1966, 109–129.

Dimensions of conflict behavior within nations, 1946–59. *Journal of Conflict Resolution* 10 (1), 1966: 65–73.

A foreign conflict behavior code sheet. *World Politics* 18(2), 1966: 283–296.

Some dimensions in the foreign behavior of nations. *Journal of Peace Research* 3(3), 1966: 201–223.

Review of Myron Weiner, ed.: Modernization—Dynamics of Growth. *American Political Science Review* 61(3), 1967: 833.

Some attributes and behavioral patterns of nations. *Journal of Peace Research* 4(2), (1967): 196–206.

Dimensions of dyadic war, 1820–52. *Journal of Conflict Resolution* 11(2), 1967: 176–183.

Understanding factor analysis. *Journal of Conflict Resolution* 11(4), 1967: 444–480.

Future research on the Asian system, *East-West Center Review* 4(2), 1967: 31–33.

The relationship between national attributes and foreign conflict. In: *Quantitative International Politics.* Edited by J David Singer. New York: Free Press, 1968, 187–214 + refs. 359–374.

Progress in understanding international relations: The DON project. *East-West Center Review* 4(3), 1968: 15–25.

Delineating international patterns and profiles. In: *The Computer and the Policy Making Community.* Edited by Davis B Bobrow & Judah L Schwartz. Englewood, Cliffs, NJ: Prentice Hall, 1969, 154–202.

Some empirical findings on nations and their behavior. *World Politics* 21(2), 1969: 226–241.

Indicators of cross-national and international patterns. *American Political Science Review* 63(1), 1969: 127–147.

Forecasting international relations: A proposed investigation of three-mode factor analysis. *Technological Forecasting* 1(2), 1969: 197–216.

Dimensions of foreign and domestic conflict behavior: A review of empirical findings. In: Theory and Research on the Causes of War. Edited by Dean G Pruitt & Richard C Snyder. Englewood Cliffs, NJ: Prentice Hall, 1969, 219–228.

Patterns of dyadic foreign conflict for 1963 (with Dennis Hall). *Multivariate Behavioral Research* 5(3), 1970: 275–293.

Course grades. *PS* 3(2), 1970: 193–195.

Issue dimensions in the 1963 United Nations General Assembly (with Richard Pratt). *Multivariate Behavioral Research* 6(3), 1971: 251–286.

Dimensions of error in cross-national data, In: *Handbook of Method in Cultural Anthropology.* Edited by Raoul Naroll & Ronald Cohen. Garden City, NY: Natural History Press, 1971, 946–961.

US foreign relations: conflict, cooperation, and attribute distances. In: *Peace, War and Numbers.* Edited by Bruce Russett. Beverly Hills, CA: Sage, 1972, 71–113.

Social time and international relations. In: *Locational Approaches to Power and Conflict.* Edited by Kevin R Cox et al. Beverly Hills, CA: Sage, 1974, 73–105.

Review of J David Singer & Melvin Small: The Wages of War, 1816–1965—A Statistical Handbook. *American Political Science Review* 69(1), 1975: 390–391.

The roots of faith. In: *In Search of Global Patterns.* Edited by James N Rosenau. New York: Free Press, 1976, 10–30.

Will the Soviet Union soon have a first-strike capability? *Orbis* 20(3), 1976: 579–594.

…Or imminent threat. *New Guard* 17 (December 1976): 14–15.

The Dimensionality of Nations Project. In: *Quantitative International Politics.* Edited by Francis W Hoole & Dina A Zinnes. New York: Praeger, 1976, 149–154.

Comments on the reviews of the Dimensionality of Nations Project. *Ibid.,* 219–243.

Détente and reality. *Strategic Review* IV (Fall 1976), 33–43.

Wishful thinking is no defense. *Reason* 9 (July 1977), 22–25.

Predicting the condo market (with Gary D Murfin). *CONDO: Honolulu Condo Report* 2 (April 22, 1977), 11–14.

Patterns and prediction equations: What are the questions? What are the uses? (with Gary D Murfin). *Ibid.* 2 (May 20, 1977), 11–15.

Patterns and prediction equations: analyzing results (with Gary D Murfin). *Ibid.* 2 (June 17, 1977), 12–14.

How multinational analyze political risk (with David A Heenan). *Harvard Business Review* 56 (January–February 1978) 67–76.

A warning on Michael Haas's International Conflict. *Journal of Conflict Resolution* 22 (1), 1978: 157–162. [Followed by a response by Michael Haas: 163–164.]

Controlling arms control: The price of peace with freedom. *Journal of International Relations* 3 (Spring 1978) 12–27.

International transactions and conflict: Polarities or complements? In: *Bonds without Bondage: Explorations in Transcultural Interactions.* Edited by Krishna Kumar. Honolulu, HI: University Press of Hawaii, 1979, 283–292.

Preparing for war? The Third Reich versus the Soviet Union today. *International Security Review* 4(Fall), 1979: 207–229.

Korea and the correlation of forces toward war. *Korea & World Affairs* 5(Spring), 1981: 18–35.

Government, violence, and social justice in Hawaii. In: 1980 Humanities Conference, Honolulu, HI: Hawaii Committee for the Humanities, 1981.

Wiberg's review essay on Rummel: A reply. *Journal of Peace Research* 20(3), 1983: 279–280.

The freedom factor. *Reason* (July), 1983: 32–38.

Libertarianism and international violence. *Journal of Conflict Resolution* 27(1), 1983: 27–71.

Libertarianism, violence within states, and the polarity principle. *Comparative Politics* 16 (4), 1984: 443–462.

Empirical basis of defense policy. In: *Defending a Free Society.* Edited by Robert W Poole, Jr. Lexington, KY: Lexington Books, 1984, 33–56.

Current strategic realities. *Ibid.* 57–97.

On fostering a just peace. *International Journal on World Peace* 1(1), 1984: 4–15.

Rummel responds to Martindale [debate about 'On fostering a just peace']. *International Journal on World Peace* 2(1), 1985: 83–85.

Freedom and global peace, *Encyclopedia of Peace*, 2, 1985.

The conflict helix. *Journal of Peace Studies* 5(December), 1985: 41–92.

Libertarian propositions on violence within and between nations: A test against published research results. *Journal of Conflict Resolution* 29(3), 1985: 419–455.

Social field theory, libertarianism, and violence. *International Journal on World Peace* 3 (4), 1986: 9–44.

Social field theory, libertarianism, and violence—rejoinder. *International Journal on World Peace* 3(4), 1986: 47–49.

This week's citation classic: Applied Factor Analysis. *Current Contents* (24), 1987: 16.

A catastrophe theory model of the conflict helix, with tests. *Behavioral Science* 32(4), 1987: 241–266.

Triadic struggle and accommodation in perspective. In: *The Strategic Triangle: China, the United States and the Soviet Union.* Edited by Ilpyong Kim. New York: Paragon House, 1987, 253–278.

On Vincent's view of freedom and international conflict. *International Studies Quarterly* 31(1), 1987: 113–125.

Deadlier than war. *IPA Review* 41, 1987:24–30.

As though a nuclear war: The death toll of absolutism. *International Journal on World Peace* 5(3), 1988: 27–44.

Roots of faith II. In: *Journeys through World Politics*. Edited by Joseph Kruzel & James N Rosenau. Lexington, KY: Lexington Books, 1989, 311–328.

Now, there's a kinder, gentler argument in favor of a free press. *ASNE Bulletin* [ASNE: American Society of Newspaper Editors] (February), 1989: 27.

War isn't this century's biggest killer. In: *International Relations*. Edited by George Lopez & Michael Stohl. Washington, DC: CQ Press, 1989: 473–476.

American troops in Korea and the potential for war. In: US Forces in Korea [in Korean]. Edited by Tong Whan Park. Seoul, Korea: Korea Institute for Defense Analysis, 1990.

Political perception, latent functions, and social fields: a quantum theory approach to politics. In: *Quantum Politics: Applying Quantum Theory to Political Phenomena*. Edited by Theodore Becker. New York: Praeger, 1991, 101–125.

Political systems, violence, and war. In: Approaches to Peace: An Intellectual Map. Edited by W Scott Thompson & Kenneth M Jensen, with Richard N Smith & Kimber M Schraub. Washington, DC: United States Institute of Peace, 1991, 347–370, including discussion. Also published as: The politics of cold blood. *Society* 27 (1), 1989: 32–40 and at http://www.firearmsandliberty.com/rummel.war.html.

The death toll of Marxism in the Soviet Union. *Internet on the Holocaust and Genocide* 30(1), 1991: 9–12.

The rule of law: towards eliminating war. Speech given to the ABA National Security Conference on The Rule of Law in United States Foreign Policy and the New World Order. Washington, DC, 10–11 October 1991.

Megamurders. *Society* 29(6), 1992: 47–52.

Power kills; absolute power kills absolutely. *Internet on the Holocaust and Genocide* 31 (June), 1992: 1–10.

Power, genocide, and mass murder. *Journal of Peace Research* 31(1), 1994: 1–10.

Democide in totalitarian states: mortacracies and megamurderers. In: *Genocide: A Critical Bibliographic Review*. Edited by Israel W Charny. Rutgers, NJ: Transaction, 1994.

Waging peace through democracy. *Waging Peace Bulletin* 4(Winter) 1994/95.

Democracy, power, genocide, and mass murder. *Journal of Conflict Resolution* 39(1), 1995: 3–26.

Democracies ARE less warlike than other regimes. *European Journal of International Relations* 1(4), 1995: 457–479.

The Holocaust in comparative and historical perspective. In: *Contemporary Genocides: Causes, Cases, Consequences*. Edited by Albert J Jongman. Leiden: PIOOM, 1996, 17–33.

Human Rights. In: *Protest, Power, and Change: An Encyclopedia of Nonviolence Action from Act-Up to Women's Suffrage*. Edited by William Vogele & Roger Powers. Hamden, CT: Garland, 1997, 232–236.

Democratization. *Ibid*: 142–145.

Is collective violence correlated with social pluralism? *Journal of Peace Research* 34(2), 1997: 163–175.

One-thirteenth of a data point does not a generalization make: A response to Dulić. *Journal of Peace Research* 41(1), 2004: 103–104.

13.2.3 Research Reports of the Dimensionality of Nations Project

Comprehensive lists of all the research reports from the DON Project are found in Hilton
(1973) and in Rummel (1976f). All the reports with Rummel as a (co-)author are
included in the following list, except those later published as articles and a few early
items (reports 3–6) mainly reporting variable lists (cf Hilton, 1973: 74).[1]

Measures of international relations (8), 1967,

The DON Project: a five-year research program (9), 1967.

The patterns of dyadic foreign conflict behavior for 1963 (with Dennis Hall) (12), 1968.

Attribute and behavioral spaces of nations: variables and samples for 1950 (13), 1968.

Estimating missing data (with Charles Wall) (20), 1969.

Foreign conflict patterns and types for 1963 (with Gary Oliva) (22), 1969.

Dynamic patterns of nation's conflict, 1955 to 1963 (with Willard Keim) (27), 1969.

Field theory and indicators of international behavior (29), 1969.

The DON Project: policy relevance and overview (34), 1969.

Field and attribute theories of nation behavior (31), 1969.

Forecasting international relations: some views on the relevancy of the Dimensionality of
Nations Project to policy planning (with Warren Phillips) (36), 1969.

Testing field theory on the 1963 behavior space of nations (with Richard Van Atta) (43),
1970.

Field theory and the 1963 space of nations (44), 1970.

Status field theory and international relations (50), 1971.

Attributes of nations: data and codes 1950–65 (with Sang-Woo Rhee & George Omen)
(65), 1973.

Behaviors of nation-dyads: data and codes 1950–65 (with Sang-Woo Rhee & George
Omen) (67), 1973.

A summary and annotated bibliography of research by the Dimensionality of Nations
Project, 1967–73 (69), 1975.

13.2.4 Papers (Department of Political Science, University of Hawaii)

Dynamics of conflict behavior, 1969, 20 pp

International social indicators and linkages, 1974, 45 pp

Conflict watch: a continuous computer monitor of the Asia-Pacific region, 1975, 46 pp

The plight of South Korea, 1975, 9 pp

Factors of crime, criminality and enforcement in Honolulu: concepts paper, 1975, 3 pp

Population policy and demographic change, 1975, 52 pp

Political systems and war, 1975, 25 pp

Synoptic computer projection of the policy environment, 1976, 70 pp

---

[1]For a reference to Hilton (1973), see the reference section of Chap. 1.

Knee–jerk negativism: the intellectual and the B-1, 1976, 8 pp
Roots of struggle, 1976, 14 pp
Assessing political risk, 1977, 36 pp
What price inferiority, 1977, 18 pp
The statistical dynamics of the US/USSR military balance, 1977, 57 pp
The probability of a Soviet-American war as judged by scientific findings on peace and
    war, 1978, 77 pp
Is deterrence collapsing? 1979, 100 pp
Fundamental and applied principles of peace and conflict, 1979, 90 pp
The new danger of a Soviet-American war, 1979, 87 pp
Freedom, violence and war, 1982, 15 pp
How many did communist regimes murder?, 1993, 3 pp
Genocide and mass murder: How many have been killed and why? 1993, 8 pp
Genocide and mass murder: The black hole in peace research, 1993, 17 pp.

13.2.5   Papers Written for the Website

Democide versus genocide. Which is what?, May 1998, at: http://www.hawaii.edu/
    powerkills/GENOCIDE.HTM.
Democide since World War II, April 1999, at: http://www.hawaii.edu/powerkills/
    POSTWWII.HTM.
Statistics of Poland's democide: Addenda, November 2000, at: http://www.hawaii.
    edu/powerkills/SOD.CHAP7.ADDENDA.HTM.
Eliminating democide and war through an alliance of democracies, June 2000, at:
    http://www.hawaii.edu/powerkills/ALLIANCE.HTM.
For shorter commentaries, see the archive on the commentary theme page, at: http://
    www.hawaii.edu/powerkills/COMMENTARY.HTM.

13.2.6   Newspaper Articles

- Testing paths to peace, *Honololu Star-Bulletin,* 27 January 1975: A–16.
- American credibility, *Honololu Star-Bulletin*, 8 April 1975.
- Kissinger versus Solzhenitsyn, *Honololu Star-Bulletin* 25 July, 1975: A–19.
- The myth of a Soviet-US arms race, *Honololu Star-Bulletin.*
- The myth of American military superiority, *Honololu Star-Bulletin* 9 August
  1975: A–10.
- Detente and the Russian threat, *Honololu Star-Bulletin* 6 January 1976: A–15.
- Overkill in military arguments, *Honololu Star-Bulletin* 15 May 1976: A–11.
- The balance of power in Asia, *Korean Herald New Year Supplement* 1 January
  1977: 5.
- The meaning of 'Roots', *Honololu Star-Bulletin* 19 February 1977: A–8.

- The question is war or peace, *Honololu Star-Bulletin* 1 February 1980: A–19.
- A scenario on unilateral disarmament, *Honololu Star-Bulletin* 18 November 1981: A–16.
- Arming Japan would foster world peace, *Press Telegram* 25 May 1984.
- Democracies don't fight each other, *Honololu Star-Bulletin* 21 June 1985.
- War isn't this century's biggest killer. *Wall Street Journal* 7 July 1986.

Rudolph J. Rummel

Rudolph Joseph Rummel (1932–2014), BA and MA from the University of Hawaii (1959, 1961); Ph.D. in Political Science (Northwestern University, 1963); Phi Beta Kappa, Phi Kappa Phi, Omicron Delta Kappa. Taught at Indiana University (1963), Yale (1964–66), University of Hawaii (1966–1995); Professor Emeritus of Political Science, University of Hawaii (1996–2014). Received numerous grants from NSF, ARPA, and the United States Peace Research Institute. Frequently nominated for the Nobel Peace Prize. Received the Susan Strange Award of the International Studies Association for having intellectually most challenged the field in 1999; the Lifetime Achievement Award 2003 from the Conflict Processes Section, American Political Science Association; and the 2007 The International Association of Genocide Scholars' Award for Distinguished Lifetime Contribution to the Field of Genocide and Democide Studies and Prevention.

Wrote about two-dozen books and over 100 professional articles. Most recent books: *Death By Government* (Transaction Publications, 1994), *The Miracle That Is Freedom* (Martin Institute for Peace Studies and Conflict Resolution, University of Idaho, 1996), *Power Kills* (Transaction Publications, 1997), and *Statistics of Democide* (Center for National Security Law, 1997). Through his undergraduate term papers, MA Thesis, Ph.D. dissertation, and academic career, R.J. Rummel has focused his research on the causes and conditions of collective violence and war with a view toward helping their resolution or elimination. He published his major results in *Understanding Conflict and War*, Vols. 1–5 (Sage Publications, 1975, 1976, 1977, 1979, and 1981). His conclusion was that "To eliminate war, to restrain violence, to nurture universal peace and justice, is to foster freedom (liberal

© The Editor(s) (if applicable) and The Author(s) 2017
N.P. Gleditsch (ed.), *R.J. Rummel: An Assessment of His Many Contributions*,
SpringerBriefs on Pioneers in Science and Practice 37,
DOI 10.1007/978-3-319-54463-2

democracy)." Given the supreme importance of this conclusion published in 1981, Rummel then spent the next fifteen years refining the underlying theory and testing it empirically on new data, against the empirical results of others, and on case studies (as in his *Death By Government*). All this theoretical, empirical, and comparative research is documented in his final work, *Power Kills*, nominated for the 1998 Grawemeyer Award for Ideas Improving World Order. *Power Kills* sums up Rummel's research on violence and reaffirms and extends his earlier work. In theory and fact, democracies do not (or virtually never) make war on each other; the more democratic two regimes, the less likely violence between them; the more democratic a regime, the less its overall foreign violence; and the more democratic a regime, the less its genocide and mass murder (which in this century has killed about four times the battle dead of all its foreign and domestic wars). With the growing international interest and work on human security, in his latest work Rummel has documented and shown empirically that the power of freedom to improve human affairs extends as well to social and economic development, Not only is democratic freedom a method of nonviolence, it also is a means to wealth and prosperity. He shows, for example, that democracies never have a famine. He also goes beyond establishing these utilitarian benefits and shows that freedom is the basic right that people have aside from however it improves their lives. He has published the results of this research exclusively on this site as *Saving Lives, Enriching Life*. In sum, then, all this research shows that democracy is a method of nonviolence—that power kills—and that freedom is not only a right, but that freedom also is an engine of wealth and prosperity. *This research thus contributes to world order by showing empirically, historically, and theoretically that fostering liberal democracy is a route to global human security.*

Source https://www.hawaii.edu/powerkills/PERSONAL.HTM.

A book website with additional information on Rummel is found at: http://afes-press-books.de/html/SpringerBriefs_PSP_Rummel.htm.

Nils Petter Gleditsch

Nils Petter Gleditsch (born 17 July 1942 in Sutton, Surrey, UK) is a Norwegian peace researcher and political scientist. He is Research Professor at the Peace Research Institute Oslo (PRIO). In 2009, Nils Petter Gleditsch was given the *Award for Outstanding Research* by the Research Council of Norway. In 1982 he was convicted (with Owen Wilkes) in Norway of a violation of the national security paragraphs of the penal code and given a suspended prison sentence. After studies in philosophy and economics Gleditsch became mag.art. in sociology at the University of Oslo. In 1966–67 he read sociology, social psychology, and international relations at the University of Michigan. Since 1964, Gleditsch has worked at the Peace Research Institute Oslo (PRIO), first as a student, later as researcher. He was Director of PRIO in 1972 and 1977–78. From 2002–08 he led the working group 'Environmental Factors of Civil War' at PRIO's Centre for the Study of Civil War, appointed as a Centre of Excellence by the Research Council of Norway. Since 1993 he has also been a part-time Professor at NTNU. Gleditsch was editor of Journal of Peace Research 1983–2010. He served as President for the International Studies Association (ISA) 2008–09. He is a member of the Royal Norwegian Society of Sciences and Letters (DKNVS) and the Norwegian Academy of Science and Letters (DNVA).

Among his books in English are: (co-ed., 1980): *Johan Galtung. A Bibliography of His Scholarly and Popular Writings 1951–80;* (with O Wilkes, 1987): *Loran-C and Omega. A Study of the Military Importance of Radio Navigation Aid*; (co-ed. with O Njølstad, 1990); *Arms Races—Technological and Political Dynamics*; (co-author with O Bjerkholt; Å Cappelen, 1994): *The Wages of Peace. Disarmament in a Small Industrialized Economy*; (co-ed. with O Bjerkholt; Å Cappelen; RP Smith; JP Dunne,

N.P. Gleditsch (ed.), *R.J. Rummel: An Assessment of His Many Contributions*,
SpringerBriefs on Pioneers in Science and Practice 37,
DOI 10.1007/978-3-319-54463-2

1996: *The Peace Dividend*; (co-ed. with L Brock; T Homer-Dixon; R Perelet; E Vlachos, 1997): *Conflict and the Environment*; (co-ed. with G Lindgren; N Mouhleb; S Smit; I de Soysa, 2000): *Making Peace Pay: A Bibliography on Disarmament and Conversion*; (co-ed. with P Diehl, 2001) *Environmental Conflict*; (co-ed. with G Schneider; K Barbieri 2003): *Globalization and Armed Conflict*; (co.ed. with G Schneider, 2013): *Assessing the Capitalist Peace.* He has also been guest-ed. and co-ed. of special journal issues including: *European Journal of International Relations,* 1(4): 405–574; *Political Geography* 26(6): 627–735; *International Studies Review* 12(1): 1–104; *International Interactions* 36(2): 107–213; *Conflict Management and Peace Science* 28(1): 5–85; *International Interactions* 38(4): 375–569; *Journal of Peace Research* 49(1): 1–267; *International Studies Perspectives* 13 (3): 211–234; *International Studies Review* 15(3): 396–419.

Website at PRIO: http://www.prio.org/staff/npg.
Website at NTNU: http://www.ntnu.edu/employees/nilspg.
Website on the editor is at: http://afes-press-books.de/html/SpringerBriefs_PSP_Gleditsch.htm.

About this Book

The book provides a critical and constructive assessment of the many contributions to social science and politics made by Professor R.J. Rummel. Rummel was a prolific writer and an important teacher and mentor to a number of people who in turn have made their mark on the profession. His work has always been controversial. But after the end of the Cold War, his views on genocide and the democratic peace in particular have gained wide recognition in the profession. He was also a pioneer in the use of statistical methods in international relations. His work in not easily classified in the traditional categories of international relations research (realism, idealism, and constructivism). He was by no means a pacifist and his views on the US Soviet arms race led him to be classified as a hawk. But his work on the democratic peace has become extremely influential among liberal IR scholars and peace researchers. Above all, he was a libertarian.

- Rummel's work on the democratic peace is key to the understanding of international relations in the post-Cold War era
- His work on a broad conception of genocide and politicide (which he defined as democide) is pioneering and remains unrivalled in the comprehensiveness of his data collection
- The contributions to this volume are by well-known scholars and (except possibly one) original for this volume.

Contents
Introduction: R.J. Rummel—A Multi-faceted Scholar (*Nils Petter Gleditsch*)—Dad (*Dawn Akemi*)—R.J. Rummel, Citizen Scholar: An Interview on the Occasion of His Retirement (*Doug Bond*)—Rummel as a Great Teacher (*Sang-Woo Rhee*)—Contextualizing Rummel's Field Theory (*Richard Chadwick*)—R.J. Rummel, Nuclear Superiority, and the Limits of Détente (*Matthew Kroenig and Bardia Rahmani*)—Rummel's Unfinished Legacy: Reconciling Peace Research and Realpolitik (*Erich Weede*)—Understanding Conflict and War: An Overlooked

© The Editor(s) (if applicable) and The Author(s) 2017
N.P. Gleditsch (ed.), *R.J. Rummel: An Assessment of His Many Contributions*,
SpringerBriefs on Pioneers in Science and Practice 37,
DOI 10.1007/978-3-319-54463-2

Classic? (*James Lee Ray*)—Rummel and Singer, DON and COW (*Frank Whelon Wayman*)—Regime Type Matters (*H.-C. Peterson*)—Democracy as a Method of Nonviolence (*Erica Chenoweth*)—The Comparative Analysis of Mass Atrocities and Genocide (*Barbara Harff*)—Curriculum Vitae and Publications.

A book website with additional information on Prof. R.J. Rummel is found at: http://afes-press-books.de/html/SpringerBriefs_PSP_Rummel.htm. A website with additional information on the editor, Prof. Nils Petter Gleditsch, and his two affiliations at PRIO in Oslo and at NTNU in Trondheim, Norway is at: http://afes-press-books.de/html/SpringerBriefs_PSP_Gleditsch.htm.